THE CHOSEN

ANONYMOUS

GARRETT J KELLAS

First edition 2026

Copyright Registration No: TXu 2-529-821
Library of Congress Control Number: 2026910671
ISBN: 979-8-9949743-1-5 (paperback)

www.spiritualdementia.com

"The craving for something more was the equivalent, on a low level, of the spiritual thirst of our being for wholeness, expressed in medieval language: the union with God."

— CARL JUNG, 1961

"Spiritum contra spiritum"—spirit against spirit.

CONTENTS

A Note Before We Begin

I did not choose to write this book. This book chose me. Ancient texts do not wait on shelves for discovery; they come to you when you are prepared to see them.

It was born the way fire is born—because the conditions demanded it. I sat down because I could not stop thinking about an ancient text— older than the Bible and rooted in the Egyptian wisdom tradition that predates Moses—that described my life with more precision than any therapist, guide, or diagnostic manual ever had. The Corpus Hermeticum VII—a short, fierce, ancient sermon about waking up from the sleep of ignorance—read like it was written by someone who had been to the rooms. The words read as though they were written by someone who had personally experienced the illusion. Someone who had walked through the door.

I penned this book for those who have overcome it yet remain unaware of what lies beyond it.

I wrote it for the ones who woke up and then realized that recovery was only the beginning—that the real work, the real stripping, the real awakening was still ahead. I wrote it for the ones who sense that the ancient instructions— trust God, clean house, help others—

are not just a program for managing symptoms. They are a program for waking up. This is a program that encourages individuals to shed their outer layers and embrace the light.

I wrote it for those mystics who are unaware of their own mystical nature. I wrote it for the seekers who believe their suffering is exclusive to them. This book is intended for those who experience the depths of their suffering on a daily basis yet lacks a language to express their emotions.

This book is in that language.

It is not a scholarly work. I am not a scholar. It is not a theological argument. I am not a theologian. It is the testimony of a man who drank himself to the edge of death, was pulled back by grace, and then spent years discovering that the ancient wisdom traditions had been describing the exact same journey all along—the same flood, the same guide, the same covering, the same door.

You do not need to belong to any tradition or practice to read this book. You do not need to be in recovery or carry any diagnosis. You do not need to know the Corpus Hermeticum, Jungian psychology, or believe in God. You need only one thing: the willingness to consider that the life you have been living might be a set and that there might be a door hidden in the painted sky.

This book is about the human condition. This book is not about addiction, even though addiction is one of its most prominent symptoms. The disease I describe in these pages is older than any substance and wider than any diagnosis. It is the disease of forgetting who you are. It afflicts executives in their corner offices, mothers at their kitchen tables, and teenagers staring at screens at three in the morning. It afflicts the religious and the secular, the successful and the failing, the young and the old. The flood described by the ancient Hermetic text does not ask whether you drink from a bottle or from the world itself. It carries everyone. And the door out is available to everyone. My doorway happened to be addiction. Yours may be the spiritual emptiness of discovering that nothing on the outside can give you fulfillment or the quiet suffocation of a life that looks fine on the outside and is dying within. The door does not care how you arrive. It only asks that you walk through.

If you have that willingness—even a sliver of it, even a whisper— then this book is for you.

Read it slowly. Read it with your chest, not just with your eyes. Let it sit. Let it stir. And if something in these pages wants to remember rather than learning, pay attention to that. That is the signal. That is the Spirit recognizing itself.

The door is open.

What I ask of you is this: suspend your certainty. You do not need to believe what I believe. You can reject the Hermetic tradition, disagree with Jung, and decline any theology whatsoever. I ask that you read with your instinct before your mind can argue. The part that recognizes truth the way a compass recognizes north— not through analysis, but through alignment.

If something on these pages feels true, let it be. Do not let the mind talk you out of what the heart has already recognized. The mind is brilliant. The mind is powerful. The mind can construct arguments against any truth that threatens its sovereignty. But the heart knows what the mind cannot calculate. And the heart, in my experience, has never lied to me. It has confused me. It has frightened me. It has led me to places the mind said were dangerous. But it has never lied.

It is wonderful to meet you at this juncture of your path. Now let us take a walk together.

Garrett J Kellas

The Door in the Painted Sky

There is a scene at the end of The Truman Show that never leaves you.

Truman has spent his entire life inside a fiction. The sky is a ceiling. The people around him are actors. Every sunrise, every relationship, every moment of his existence has been scripted, produced, and broadcast for an audience he does not know is watching. He eats breakfast in a kitchen designed by strangers. He drives to work on roads that lead nowhere beyond the edges of the set. He kisses his wife goodnight without knowing she was hired for the role. Every aspect of his life—his experiences, the weather, the obstacles, and the triumphs—has been manufactured for entertainment.

But something in him always sensed the edges. The cracks. The way the light fell wrong sometimes. The way people repeated themselves. A stage light falling from the sky and being explained away as airplane debris. His father appearing on the street after being declared dead. There was a persistent, nameless feeling that there was more, something beyond what he could see, and something just outside the frame.

And then one day, his boat hits the wall.

The horizon he had been sailing toward— the endless possibility he believed in—turns out to be paint on plaster. The sky is a ceiling. The world has a boundary. Everything he thought was real was a set. The ocean he was sailing across was a shallow tank on a soundstage.

He finds the stairs. He climbs. And at the top, there is a door.

Just a simple door, hidden in the painted sky.

The creator of the show—Christof— speaks to him from above. A voice from the heavens, but not God. A false god. The architect of his prison. Christof tells Truman there is no more truth out there than in the world he created for him. Same lies. Same deceit. But in his world, Truman has nothing to fear.

Stay inside. Stay comfortable. Stay asleep. The final argument.

I have heard that voice. I have heard it in my own head a thousand times. The voice that says the unknown is worse than the known. The voice that says the prison you can predict is safer than the freedom you cannot. The voice that says stay—stay numb, stay small, stay asleep, stay where I can control you.

Truman listens. Pauses. He looks up at the voice that has controlled his entire life. And you can see the moment it happens— the moment the spell breaks. He does not argue with Christof. He does not debate. He simply recognizes that the voice, however powerful, however persuasive, however godlike in its authority, is not God. It is the creator of a prison, not the creator of a world.

Then he turns to the door. He bows—not in defeat, but in farewell. He honors the place he is leaving. He acknowledges the world that raised him, the set that shaped him, and the life that brought him to this threshold.

And he walks through.

He does not know what is on the other side. He does not ask for proof. He does not wait for a sign. He does not demand to see the net before he jumps. He does not consult a committee or read a book about walking through doors or attend an online seminar on the theological implications of thresholds.

He just opens the door and steps into the unknown.

I want to pause on the word "unknown," because it is the word that separates the awake from the asleep. The asleep require knowledge. They require certainty. They require the guarantee that what lies ahead is better than what lies behind before they will take a single step. And because no such guarantee exists—because the nature of the door is that you cannot see through it until you have walked through it—the asleep stay where they are. They stay inside. They stay in the scripts. They stay in the beautiful, comfortable, suffocating certainty of a life they can predict.

The awake walk into the unknown. Not because they are fearless—they are terrified. Not because they know what awaits them—they know nothing. But because they know, with a knowledge that does not come from the mind, that the known has failed them. It has failed them. The scripts have failed them. The certainty has failed them. And the only thing left—the only thing the false self has not ruined, has not coopted, has not swallowed undiluted and vomited back up—is the unknown.

The unknown is where God lives. Not in the certainty. Not in the doctrine. Not in the theology or the philosophy or the perfectly articulated program. God lives in the space between the door and whatever is on the other side of it. God lives in the gap. God lives in the leap. God lives in the moment when you stop demanding to know and start being willing not to know.

That is faith. Not the belief in propositions. Not the subscription to a creed. Faith is the willingness to walk into the unknown because the known has failed you. Faith is the step through the door. Faith is Truman's bow and farewell and the soft click of a door opening and the first breath of air from the other side.

That moment is the axis on which this entire book turns. Not the suffering that came before. Not the light that comes after. The moment of stepping through. The moment of choosing the unknown over the known. The moment of trusting the door more than the familiar one.

I replay this scene in my mind often because it mirrors the central act of recovery with an accuracy that borders on prophecy. Every person who wakes up makes Truman's choice. Every soul who walks toward the door for the first time is standing at the top of those stairs, looking at a door they cannot see through, hearing a voice from above that tells them to stay where it is safe. Every single one of them must make the same decision Truman made: Do I stay in the world I know, or do I walk into the one I do not?

The remarkable thing is how many people choose the door. Broken, desperate, shaking, and out of options—they choose the unknown. They choose it not because they are brave but because they have exhausted every alternative. It has all failed them. The scripts have failed them. The painted sky has cracked, and through the cracks, they can feel something that feels more real than anything ever offered.

That feeling is what I call the breeze through the door. You cannot see what is on the other side, but you can feel the air. And the air from the other side is clean. It carries a scent you have never smelled but somehow recognize. It whispers of a world you have never visited but somehow remember. And that feeling—that faint, unmistakable sensation of home—is enough to make you step through.

The audience watching the show—people in bars, in living rooms, on couches—erupts in cheering. For a moment, they are moved. They saw something real. A man chose freedom over comfort. A man walked into the unknown rather than remain in a beautiful lie.

Then someone asks what else is on.

They change the channel.

I think about this all the time. The audience does not walk through the door. They watch someone else walk through it, they are briefly moved, and then they return to the program. They consume the awakening as entertainment and learn nothing from it. The liberation is content. The transformation is a show. They applaud the freedom and remain in their chairs.

This is the condition of the spiritual consumer. The person who reads about enlightenment but does not practice it. The person who attends retreats, workshops, and seminars and collects certificates of awareness without ever being aware. The person who knows all the right words—surrender, presence, dissolution of self, non-attachment—and cannot sit in silence for five minutes without reaching for their phone.

I was this person. For a while, I was this person even in recovery. I attended meetings like I attended movies—absorbing the content, appreciating the performances, and leaving unchanged. It was not until someone grabbed me by the collar—metaphorically, but with the force of someone who meant it—and said, "This is not entertainment; this is your life," that I understood the difference between watching the door and walking through it.

The door is not a show. The door is a threshold. And thresholds are not for watching. They are for crossing.

That is humanity. Entertained by awakening, then moving on. Consuming liberation as content. Watching someone else walk through the door and feeling, briefly, the pull—then settling back into the couch. The false reality is comfortable. The scripts are familiar. The channel can always be changed.

But there is another audience. One the movie does not show.

"There is rejoicing in the presence of the angels of God over one sinner who repents." — (Luke 15:10)

Behind the painted sky, beyond the illusion, the real witnesses are not fickle. They have been watching the whole time. Through every stumble, every forgetting, every near miss.

Patient. Hoping. And when the door finally opens—

Rejoicing.

Not because Truman performed well. Not because he earned it. Not because he passed a test. Because he came home. Because the thing that was lost was found. Because the prodigal, after wandering through every country of the inner deceiver, finally turned his face toward the father's house.

This book is about the door.

It is about the world I lived in—the invisible one—the one I could sense but could not name. The reality that everyone around me accepted without question. The people followed the scripts without knowing they were scripts. The painted sky I thought was real because I had never sailed far enough to touch it.

It is about the cracks. I noticed. The moments when something felt wrong. When the light fell differently. When someone said something that did not match the script. When I caught, out of the corner of my eye, the edge of the set—the place where the floor met the wall and the dream frayed.

It is about the voice that told me to stay inside. The false comfort of the familiar prison. The voice, dressed as God, speaking from above, promised safety in exchange for my surrender to sleep. The voice that said, "You cannot survive out there." The voice that said, "This is all there is." The voice that said, sit down, shut up, and accept the painted sky.

And it is about the door hidden in the sky. The one I could only find when I stopped believing the horizon was real. The one that leads somewhere I could not see until I stepped through.

I did not find this door through wisdom. I found it through destruction.

Collapse. Rock bottom. The complete annihilation of everything I thought I was. I sailed my boat into the wall because I had no choice—I had run out of sea. Every escape route was closed. Every detour led back to the same dead end. The substances stopped working. The distractions stopped numbing. The lie I had been living could no longer sustain its own weight, and the whole structure came down.

And when I hit the painted sky, when the world I had constructed finally cracked open, I found the stairs. Not because I was special. Not because I was chosen by some cosmic hand. Because I was desperate. Because the only thing more terrifying than the unknown was one more day inside the walls.

The rooms of recovery were my first glimpse that it was not all there was. People who had walked through before me. Guides who took my hand. A program that pointed toward a door I could not yet see. In those rooms—in church basements and community centers and hospital conference rooms—I heard my own story reflected to me in a hundred different voices. And each voice confirmed what I had begun to suspect: it was all real, and there was something beyond it.

But the rooms were the beginning, not the end. And that is the sentence that separates this book from most recovery literature.

I am deeply grateful for the rooms. They saved my life. They gave me recovery, community, a framework for understanding what had happened to me, and a set of practices that keep me grounded to this day. I do not write this book as a departure from the rooms. I write it

with dirt under my fingernails and gratitude in my chest and the absolute conviction that the ancient texts knew what they were talking about. Not as a metaphor. Not as poetry. As described. An exact, precise, experiential description of a territory that is as real as the chair you are sitting in, as tangible as the breath you are drawing, and as undeniable as the ache in your chest that brought you to this book.

There is a difference between not dying and being alive. Recovery taught me not to die. What followed taught me how to live. And the how of living—the actual, daily, embodied practice of being fully present in a world that is both broken and beautiful—is what this book is about. It is about the morning practice and the evening inventory and the moment in the middle of the afternoon when the old pattern tightens and you must choose, again, whether to let it strangle you or to rip it away. It is about the silence and what speaks in it. It is about the door and what waits behind it. It is about the long, slow, spiraling journey from the fiction to the open sky.

But somewhere around my third year of recovery, I began to sense that there was more. Not more in the sense of better—the rooms do not need improving. More in the sense of deeper. The program had cracked the illusion. It had shown me the stairs. It had placed my hand on the doorknob. But the door led somewhere that the rooms themselves did not fully describe. And I needed to go there.

This is not a criticism of recovery. This is the natural arc of the soul. Recovery is the first gate. The first gate leads to honesty, to the demolition of it. But beyond the first gate, there are more gates. More doors. More layers to remove. More levels of the flood to swim against. More rooms in the house to explore—rooms the thief never showed you, rooms filled with light you did not know existed.

The Chosen Anonymous is the name I have given to the journey beyond the first gate. The journey that begins where recovery achieves its primary purpose—keeping you alive—and continues into the territory of actually living. Not just surviving. Not just coping. Not just managing. Living. In the full, vibrant, terrifying, beautiful sense of the word.

The Hermetic text describes this territory. Jung mapped its contours. The mystics of every tradition have walked its paths. And the one cracked open by suffering and rebuilt by grace is uniquely positioned to enter it. Because they have already died once. They have already lost everything. They have already walked through the fire and come out the other side with nothing but the clothes on their back—clothes which, as it turns out, are the veil that must now be ripped away.

The rooms got me to the door. This book is about what is on the other side.

The Hermetic tradition, rooted in the ancient Egyptian wisdom that predates the biblical texts, describes the same journey. It speaks of seeking a guide to take you by the hand and lead you to the portals of knowledge. There, it says, shines the light cleansed of darkness. There is no one drunk. All are sober and gaze with the heart toward one who wishes to be seen.

I did not discover these texts until years into my recovery. And when I read them, I wept. Not because they told me something new. Because they confirmed something I had already experienced. The language was ancient, the concepts universal, and the map they drew matched the territory I had been walking through. The flood. The guide. It. The door. It was all there, written millennia ago by someone who had walked the same path.

The recovery tradition calls the moment of surrender the keystone—the central stone in the arch that holds everything else together. Without it, the structure collapses. With it, you walk through to freedom.

An arch. A gate. A door in the painted sky.

The same teaching appears across centuries, traditions, and every conceivable cultural barrier, pointing at the same threshold.

I did not seek this convergence. I stumbled into it. I was driving my truck through the Arizona desert in the middle of the night, listening to the Hermetic teaching for the first time. But I was not listening with my ears. I was hearing with the organs of sense—the deeper faculty that the text itself describes. If I had been listening with my ears, I would have missed the message entirely. Instead, I was meditating on the words, and the words were clear. Unmistakably clear. They described my life with a precision that no modern book, no counselor, and no diagnosis ever had. The same flood. The same drowning. The same desperate search for a guide. The same moment of tearing off what covered me and standing, terrified and exhilarated, in the clean light of something I could not name but recognized instantly.

Think about that. How does a man who lived a destructive life stumble into recovery, stay sober, reach further than the rooms, discover an ancient text older than the Bible, listen to it in the cab of his truck with nothing but human comprehension—and find an identical path running through the Hermetic teaching, through Jung, and through the recovery tradition? A path of self-forgetting and remembering that no one has ever mapped in this way before? That is not a coincidence. That is alignment.

I read the passage again. And again. And I began to see that the recovery path—trust God, clean house, help others—and the Hermetic sermon and Jung's map of the psyche were not three separate things converging by coincidence. There were three languages describing the same territory. Three sets of directions to the same door. Three hands pointing at the same moon.

This book is my attempt to show you the moon they are all pointing at.

Carl Jung wrote that addiction is the equivalent, on a low level, of the spiritual thirst of our being for wholeness. That single sentence reframed everything I thought I knew about my disease. The craving was never for the thing I reached for. It was for the door. The numbing was just a counterfeit key—one that promised escape from the prison but only led deeper into it. Every

drink, every hit, every fix was an attempt to dissolve the walls of the prison from the inside. And every time, the walls grew thicker.

The real key was surrender. And surrender is the one thing it cannot do. It can fight. It can negotiate. It can strategize, plan, and manage. But it cannot surrender because surrender is its death. And so, the real key—the only key that opens the door—requires the dissolution of the very part of you that has been holding all the other keys.

This is the cosmic joke at the heart of recovery, at the heart of the Hermetic teaching, at the heart of every genuine spiritual tradition. The thing you need to let go of is the thing that does the holding. The hand that must open is the hand that has been gripping. And the hand does not know how to open itself. It has been clenched for so long that the muscles of clenching have forgotten there is any other position.

Surrender is not a technique. It is a catastrophe. It is the moment when the grip fails—not because you decided to let go, but because your fingers are too broken to hold on. It is the admission that the clenching has been the problem all along, and the admission only comes when the pain of clenching exceeds the fear of releasing.

My surrender did not happen on my knees in a quiet room. It happened behind the wheel. All my resources were gone. Every bridge I had ever built was burned. I was a living corpse—the very thing the Hermetic text describes—and even my ego was giving up. I was watching the pillars of the overpasses on the freeway and having thoughts of running into one straight on. I was crying so deeply I was gasping for air. No human interaction could have saved me. No phone call. No conversation. No hand on my shoulder. I was past all of that. And then something rose from

deep in my chest—from nowhere I can explain— and these are the words that came out: Please help me. That was all. And something answered. Something heard my soul cry.

If you know this feeling—this place where hope is not just absent but irrelevant—then I am writing to you.

The real escape was death—not of the body, but of the character. The identity. The Truman who believed the painted sky was real. The pretender that had appointed itself God and was running the show into the ground.

When that Truman dies, something else is born. Something that can finally see the stairs, climb them, and walk through them.

I use the word "born" deliberately. This is not a renovation. It is not a remodeling of the existing structure. It is a birth. The thing that appears from the death of the inner resistance is not an improved version of the old self. It is a new creation. It has new eyes. New ears. New organs of belief that the old self did not know existed. It sees a world the old self could not see, hears a music the old self could not hear, and knows a love the old self could not fathom.

Recovery describes this as a psychic change—a fundamental reorganization of the inner life so total that the person who emerges is a different person. The same body, the same memories, the same address, and the same phone number. But a different being. Someone who can look at the painted sky without belief. Someone who can stand at the threshold of the door and choose, freely, without the tyranny of it pulling them back, to walk through.

Jung called it "metanoia"—a Greek word meaning a change of mind, but more accurately a change of being. A turning around. A reversal of the fundamental orientation of the psyche. The self-centered life becomes the self-centered life. The small self gives way to the larger self. And the larger Self, rooted in something the small self could never access, begins to live a life the small self could never imagine.

This is what awaits on the other side of the door. Not a better version of the prison. Not a more comfortable prison. A new life. A new birth. A new set of eyes opening for the first time in a world that is ancient and infinite and has been waiting, with the patience of love, for you to see it.

This book is not for everyone.

It is not for people who are comfortable in it. Not for people who prefer the scripts. Not for people who need to see the net before they jump. It is not an argument. I am not trying to convince anyone of anything. The illusion is comfortable, and I understand why people stay.

It is for the ones who have already hit the wall. Who have felt the plaster behind the paint. Who knows, somewhere beneath the noise, that there is a door—and they are ready to find it.

It is for the ones who woke up but kept searching. Who sensed that recovery was a beginning, not an end. Who walked through the first gate and discovered there were more. Who sat in the rooms and heard the truth but felt, in their bones, that the truth went deeper than the rooms could take them.

It is for the chosen.

Not chosen because they are special. Chosen because they are willing. Willing to leave the fabrication. Willing to stop believing the resistance dressed as God. Willing to open the door without knowing what is on the other side. Chosen by their own willingness, which is itself a form of grace.

I have come to believe that willingness is not something you generate. It is something that happens to you. It is a gift—the first gift, the gift that makes all other gifts possible. You do not decide to be willing the way you decide to go to the store. Willingness arises. It appears from the wreckage. It blooms in the soil that has been turned over by suffering.

Some people must suffer more than others before the willingness comes. Some must lose everything. Some must lose things they did not know they could lose. Some must die—not physically, but in every other way—before the willingness is born in the ashes of their old life.

I do not understand the mechanics of this. I do not know why some people find willingness after one bad night and others do not find it after a decade of bad nights. I do not know why the soil of some souls turns over quickly and the soil of others stays hard and dry for years. But I know that the willingness, when it comes, is not your doing. It is grace wearing the mask of desperation. It is God reaching through the wreckage to touch the one part of you that has not yet been destroyed.

And if you feel it now—that stirring, that readiness, that inexplicable sense that these words are landing on something that has been waiting for them—do not question it. Do not analyze it. Do not try to understand it before you act on it. Act first. Understand later. The willingness is fragile. It can fade. It can be talked out of existence by the inner voice, which will offer a thousand reasons why now is not the time and you are not the one and the familiar is fine.

It is not fine. The willingness is real. And the door is open.

The Truman Show ends with a man walking through a door.

It does not show us what is beyond it.

That is what this book is for.

The word "anonymous" carries a deeper weight than simply being unnamed. It speaks to a way of being—a life lived without self-interest, without the hunger to be recognized, applauded, or elevated. Anonymity is the soul stripped of its costumes, standing bare before the Divine with no rank, no résumé, and no performance to uphold. It is the posture of one who has surrendered the need to be anything other than what they truly are: a returning child, a witness, or a leaf carried by the wind to the place it was always meant to arrive.

I stay anonymous in my recovery not because I hide who I am but because the spirit of recovery asks for something deeper than a label. I do not need you to know the details that define me on paper. I do not need you to follow my journey or confirm my experience. My task is simply to extend my hand and trust that the right person will take it. That is the anonymity of the spirit—the willingness to serve without applause, to guide without glory, and to carry the message without needing credit.

The chosen are anonymous because the choosing has nothing to do with labels or personal merit. None of us earned our place here. It was given. And what is given freely asks only one thing in return: the willingness to pass it on.

The door is open.
The angels are watching.
And if you are reading this, you are closer than you think.
them.

1

Corpus Hermeticum VII

That the greatest evil in mankind is ignorance concerning God.

Where are you heading in your drunkenness, you people? Have you swallowed the doctrine of ignorance undiluted, vomiting it up already because you cannot hold it? Stop and sober yourselves up! Look up with the eyes of the heart - if not all of you, at least those of you who have the power. The vice of ignorance floods the whole earth and utterly destroys the soul shut up in the body, preventing it from anchoring in the havens of deliverance. [2] Surely you will not sink in this great flood? Those of you who can will take the ebb and gain the haven of deliverance and anchor there. Then, seek a guide to take you by the hand and lead you to the portals of knowledge. There shines the light cleansed of darkness. There no one is drunk. All are sober and gaze with the heart toward one who wishes to be seen, who is neither heard nor spoken of, who is seen not with the eyes but with mind and heart. But first you must rip off the tunic that you wear, the garment of ignorance, the foundation of vice, the bonds of corruption, the dark cage, the living death, the sentient corpse, the portable tomb, the resident thief, the one who hates through what he loves and envies through what he hates.

Such is the odious tunic you have put on. It strangles you and drags you down with it so that you will not hate its viciousness, not look up and see the fair vision of truth and the good that lies within, not understand the plot that it has plotted against you when it made insensible the organs of sense, made them inapparent and unrecognized for what they are, blocked up with a great load of matter and jammed full of loathsome pleasure, so that you do not hear what you must hear nor observe what you must observe.

2

Whither Stumble Ye, Sots?

*Where are you heading in your drunkenness, you
people? Have you swallowed the doctrine of ignorance
undiluted, or are you vomiting it up already because
you cannot hold it?*

— CORPUS HERMETICUM VII

I was stumbling long before I picked up a drink.

That is the part nobody tells you about. The bottle was not the beginning. It was a symptom of something that had been happening for years—a slow, aimless drift through a life I never chose. I navigated my days like a man lost in a fog, colliding with invisible walls and stumbling over things I refused to acknowledge. I called it living. I called it normal. Everyone around me was doing the same thing, so I assumed this was just what life was.

I was a child who felt too much and learned early to feel less. That is the origin story of most human suffering, if we are honest. The world was too loud, too bright, too sharp, and nobody offered me a volume knob. So, I found my own. First through avoidance— disappearing into fantasies, into distractions, into any activity that would take me out of the present moment. Then through substances. The first drink did not make me cheerful. It made me normal. It took the volume of existence and turned it down to a level I could manage. And I thought, this is what everyone else feels like all the time. This sensation is what I have been missing.

I was wrong. What I had found was not normality. It was a deeper kind of sleep. A more sophisticated numbness. It was a more rapid descent into unconsciousness.

The Hermetic text asks a pointed question. Where are you heading in your drunkenness? Not "Where have you been?" Not, how did you get here? Where are you heading? The question implies motion. We are not standing still in our ignorance. We are walking somewhere. Stumbling toward something. And we have no idea where.

I spent years heading nowhere and calling it ambition. I chased things—money, approval, pleasure, escape—without ever asking why. The momentum felt like purpose. The busyness felt like meaning. But I was a sleepwalking man in circles, convinced every step was progress. I accumulated things. I achieved things. I crossed items off lists and moved to new cities and started over and started over and started over. Each fresh start felt like a recurrent stumble in a different zip code.

The text calls us sots. Drunkards. But the intoxication it describes is not just alcohol. Alcohol was my poison, yes. But the deeper intoxication is ignorance itself—the wine of forgetting who we are. The entire world drinks it. It is served at every table. It permeates every screen, every advertisement, and every conversation, never delving deeper than the surface. We gulp it down and call it culture. We pass it to our children and call it education. We pour it into every institution—schools, corporations, governments, even churches—and we call it progress.

The wine of ignorance is not served in bars alone. It is served in boardrooms. In classrooms. Families gather in living rooms, staring at separate screens, each sipping from their own private bottle. The intoxication is universal. The hangover is collective. And the stumbling—the blind, purposeless, headlong stumbling of a species that has forgotten where it came from and has no idea where it is going—is the defining feature of human civilization.

I swallowed the doctrine of ignorance undiluted. When I first read that line, it struck me as profoundly true. Undiluted. Full strength. No mixer. No chaser. I took the lie straight—that I was my body, that my worth was measured by my accomplishments, that the material world was all there was, and that God was either a fairy tale or a distant judge who set the rules and disappeared. I drank that doctrine every day of my life and wondered why I felt sick.

The doctrine of ignorance is not a philosophy you subscribe to. It is the air you breathe. It is the assumption that underpins every other assumption. It says, "You are alone." You are a body. You are born, you suffer, you die, and there is nothing else. It says that meaning is something you make, not something you discover. It says that the universe is indifferent, that consciousness is an accident, and that the ache in your chest is a chemical imbalance and nothing more.

And then I could not hold it anymore.

That is precisely what I experienced at my lowest point. The text describes it perfectly— vomiting it up because you cannot hold it. The body rejects what was never meant to be consumed. The soul rejects the lie it was forced to swallow. Reaching the bottom is not a sign of failure. It is the body's wisdom. It is the moment the organism says no more. It is the immune system of the soul, finally kicking in after years of suppression.

I remember the night it happened for me. I will not dress it up or make it poetic. I was on the floor. I was done. Every structure I had built— every story I had told myself about who I was and why my life made sense—had collapsed. The money was gone. The relationships were gone. The health was going. And the thing I had been using to hold it all together— the numbing sensation, which had served as a great anesthetic, had now turned against me. It no longer provided relief. It only provided more pain. And in the wreckage, for the first time, I had nothing left to drink. Nothing left to swallow. Nothing left to pretend.

Jung's insight about the spiritual thirst beneath addiction was not abstract to me. It was an autobiography. The craving is not the problem. The craving is a signal. It is the soul's distress call, misdirected through the only channels it knows—numbing, sensation, and distraction. The sufferer does not reach for the numbing agent because they love it. They reach because they are dying of a thirst that nothing external can quench. The more they drink, the thirstier they get, as what they look for is not in a bottle. It lives inside a door.

I was that person. Not only was I intoxicated with alcohol, but I was also intoxicated with everything the world offered as a substitute for the real thing. Drunk on approval. Drunk on control. I was under the delusion that correct arrangement of the external circumstances in my life would alleviate the internal pain. I rearranged and rearranged, and the ache persisted. That is like trying to cure a headache by rearranging the furniture, because you cannot fix the inside by rearranging the outside.

I moved the couch of my career. I repositioned the table of my relationships. I redecorated the room of my personality. And every time I finished rearranging, I sat down in the newly arranged room and felt the exact same headache. The exact same ache. The hollow, nameless, unfixable wrongness persisted, unaffected by any external adjustments.

I was the director who insisted on controlling every scene. I was on a stage, rearranging the other actors, adjusting the lighting, rewriting the script, building, and demolishing sets—and wondering why the play never felt right. It never felt right because I was supposed to be the assistant director. I was supposed to be in the play. Not controlling it. Living it. Responding to it. I allowed it to unfold without insisting that it follow my plan.

When I stopped directing—when I finally, exhaustedly, put down the megaphone and sat in the audience—the play began to make sense. Not because it changed. It began to make sense because I ceased trying to control it. Because I stopped being the problem that disguised itself as the solution.

It never stopped.

The first honest admission in recovery is powerlessness. I resisted that word for a long time. Powerless sounded like weakness. It sounded like giving up. It sounded like the admission of a defective man in a world that rewards strength and punishes vulnerability. But I have come to understand it differently now. Powerlessness is not weakness. It is accuracy. It is the first honest assessment of the situation. I cannot control this. I cannot manage this. I cannot think my way out of a prison my thinking built. The admission of powerlessness is not the end of strength. It is the beginning of a different kind of strength—the strength to stop pretending.

Whither stumble ye, sots? Where was I going? Nowhere. I was stumbling in the dark, clutching a bottle that promised light and delivered only deeper darkness. And the most terrifying part was that I did not know I was stumbling. I thought I was walking straight. I thought the darkness was daylight. I thought the stumbling was dancing.

That is the doctrine of ignorance. Not stupidity. This does not imply a deficiency in knowledge. A fundamental forgetting. It is a forgetting so complete that you do not realize you have forgotten. You walk through the world asleep and dream that you are awake. You stumble through the dark and call it navigation.

The first step in any awakening is the admission that you have been asleep.

I was asleep. I was stumbling. I was a sot.

And then, mercifully, I could not hold it anymore.

Most people do not recognize the mercy at the bottom until they are looking back from a higher perspective. The mercy is the ending. Mercy is the point at which a lie can no longer sustain itself and collapses under its own weight.

If the lie holds, you stay its prisoner. But when it breaks—when the doctrine of ignorance, swallowed undiluted, finally comes back up—there is a clearing. A terrible, beautiful clearing. A space where something new can begin, precisely because everything old has been destroyed.

I did not opt for the lowest point. Nobody does. It chose me. Or rather, it was the inevitable result of a trajectory that could only end one way. When you swallow poison every day, the body eventually rebels. When you build your life on lies, the structure eventually falls. The collapse is not punishment. It is physics. It is the natural consequence of a design that was never meant to hold.

And in the clearing left by the collapse, for the first time in my life, I could hear. Not the noise of the world. The sound was not the chattering of the mind. Something else. There was a voice that had been speaking all along, hidden beneath the noise, beneath the drunkenness, and beneath the decades of forgetfulness. I had never been quiet enough to recognize the voice I heard.

That voice said, "There is a door." And I was desperate enough to believe it.

I want to say something about desperation, because the world treats it as a weakness and I have come to understand it as a doorway. Nobody walks through the door out of comfort. Nobody leaves because life inside it is working.

Desperation is the admission fee. It is the price of entry into the territory of the real. And the price is not too high—it is precisely right. Only the desperate have the humility to accept what the door offers. Only the desperate have been stripped of the arrogance that says, "I can do this myself."

I have met people with years of recovery who still carry themselves with the posture of self-sufficiency. They attend meetings like board meetings, checking items off lists and managing their recovery like a portfolio. And I watch them, and I recognize my old self. He was the man who believed he could think his way to God. He believed that if he accumulated enough spiritual knowledge, the transformation would happen automatically, akin to a software update. It does not work that way. The transformation is not an upgrade. It is death and rebirth. And death does not come to be comfortable. It comes to the desperate.

The mystics of every tradition knew this. The dark night of the soul is not an obstacle on the path. It is the path. The stripping, the emptying, the total annihilation of everything you thought you were—this is not a detour. This is the route. And the only people who take this route are the ones who have no other options left. These are the individuals for whom all other paths have reached a point of no return. Those desperate enough to walk into an unseen darkness, trusting that the voice they heard in the silence was a hand extended from the other side rather than a hallucination.

I was that desperate. And desperation, it turned out, was the only qualification I needed.

3

Stay Ye, Be Sober

Stop and sober yourselves up!
Look up with the eyes of the heart.

— CORPUS HERMETICUM VII

Stop!

That was the first real instruction I ever received. Do not fix yourself. Not figure it out. Do not try harder. Not read another book, attend another seminar, or develop another strategy. Stop.

The Hermetic text does not say to walk in a different direction. It does not say, "Find a better path." It says stop. Cease your stumbling. Stand still. Be sober. The first act of awakening is not movement forward. It is the cessation of the wrong movement. Before you can see where you are, you must stop running. Before you can hear the truth, you must stop talking. Before you can feel the solid ground, you must stop thrashing in the water.

I ran for years. I ran from pain. I ran from stillness. I fled silence, where the truth lived, because I could not afford to hear it. Running felt productive. Running felt like I was doing something. But running from yourself is a race you can never win because the thing chasing you lives inside your chest. You can cross oceans, and it comes with you. You can change your name, and it knows who you are. You can fill every moment with noise, and it patiently waits for the moment when the noise ceases.

I ran to new cities. I ran from new relationships. I ran to the gym, to the office, to the bar, and to the bed. I ran for anything that would keep my feet moving and my mind occupied and my soul too exhausted to speak.

And every time I stopped moving—every time the plane landed, or the party ended, or the high wore off—there it was. The silence. The ache. The presence of my own unlived life was unbearable.

When I finally stopped—when my body gave out, when my will collapsed, when I had nothing left to run on and nowhere left to run to— something happened that I did not expect. The world got quiet. It is not peaceful yet. Just be quiet. The silence is akin to the moment following a storm when the wind subsides and your own breathing becomes audible for the first time. It was akin to the pause that occurs between a flash of lightning and thunder, a moment in which everything holds its breath.

That was waking up. Not the absence of the substance—that came too, and it mattered enormously—but the deeper awakening. This was the sobriety of the mind. The moment I stopped performing, stopped managing, stopped narrating my own life, and stood still inside it. At that moment, the runner came to a halt and realized that the entity he had been escaping was not a monster. It was a mirror.

The text says, "Look up with the eyes of the heart." I did not understand that phrase for a long time. I thought the heart was just an organ, or at best a metaphor for emotion. However, the heart that the Hermeticists depict is a completely different entity. It is an organ of perception. It sees what the eyes cannot. It knows what the mind cannot calculate. It perceives itself directly, without the filters of language, logic, and self. The heart sees truth the way the eye sees color— at once, without translation, without doubt.

The heart opens its eyes. I felt them opening before I had words for what was happening. In the rooms of recovery, sitting in a folding chair in a church basement, listening to a stranger tell his story, I felt something in my chest respond. Not my brain. Not my emotions, exactly. Something deeper. Something structural. Something that had been closed for so long that I had forgotten it could open. And when it opened, with a crack, the light that came through was blinding.

I heard someone tell my story. Not the details—the details were different. He was older, from a different place, with a different story and a separate set of wreckage. But the shape of it. The architecture of it. The fleeing, falling, and lying stopped when there was no one left to lie to. And something in my chest recognized truth, the way a compass recognizes north. They did not think about it. It simply turned.

Jung called the event the moment of clarity—the instant when consciousness breaks through the fog of the unconscious. He believed that most of human life is spent in a kind of waking sleep, driven by forces we do not understand. Complexes. Shadows. We mistake inherited patterns of behavior for free will. The moment of clarity is when the conscious mind pierces through, even briefly, and sees the machinery. It sees the gears turning. It sees the puppet strings. And in that seeing, something shifts—partially, but something fundamental.

The world cracks.

Here is what I discovered, and it changed everything. Stopping the behavior and waking up from the self are not the same thing. I stopped the behavior and picked up the same self-will that drove me to the bottle in the first place. I had stopped the external behavior, but I had not woken up. I was still intoxicated by my thinking, my plans, and my own desperate need to control every outcome and manage every impression. The bottle was gone, but the bartender was still pouring.

The Hermetic call to sobriety goes deeper than the cessation of any one behavior. It is a call to wake up from the entire dream—not just the symptom, but the self that produced it. It's not just about addressing the symptom, but also about addressing the underlying disease. The false self-pours and drinks, making this intoxication subtler than any drug. You cannot use the narrator to defeat it. That is like asking the thief to guard the vault.

Stay. Be sober. Look up.

I am still learning how to do this.

But I know now what the stillness is for. It is for seeing. And you cannot see with eyes full of motion. You cannot hear with ears full of noise. You cannot know God with a mind full of yourself.

There is a practice I was taught early in recovery that I still use every day. It is simple, embarrassingly simple. When the noise begins—when the mind starts its narration, when the old anxiety fires up, when the mind begins its relentless commentary on everything that is wrong or might go wrong—I stop. Physically stop. Whatever I am doing, wherever I am, I stop. I take three breaths. Not deep, dramatic breaths. Simple, ordinary breaths. And with each breath, I let something go. The first breath releases the past—whatever regret or resentment I am carrying. The second breath releases the future— whatever fear or anticipation has gripped me. The third breath opens the present—the only moment that is happening.

It takes about fifteen seconds. It changes everything. Not permanently. Not dramatically. But enough. This level of intensity is sufficient to disrupt the state of trance. It's sufficient to disrupt the monotonous discourse. It is just enough to cause a slight crack in the garment, allowing a sliver of light to shine through.

I have taught this practice to others, and I have watched it change the quality of their days. Not dramatically. Not in the way the mind wants change to happen—all at once, permanent, complete. Real change occurs in a small, accumulative way. One breath at a time. Real change happens one breath at a time. Each day, a small crack accumulates over weeks, months, and years, until the shroud becomes thin enough for light to penetrate the skin.

I used to come home from work regularly upset and irritated from the day, then release my frustration on my loving, caring wife. I had no control over my bruised pride. I was exhausted. I was making home not a sanctuary but a place of restlessness.

One day I came home like I usually did. I walked through the front door. My wife noticed the familiar expression on my face and abruptly stopped me. She said, "Would you like to go back outside and come back in and start over and have a peaceful night?"

I did not react. I stopped. I listened. And I heard the message clearly. I went back outside to my car and took enough time for three breaths to reset. Then I went home to enjoy the peace in my house.

The practices are small. The effects are not.

The stillness is not emptiness. That is the wonderful surprise. When you stop fleeing and stand still, the silence is not vacant. It is full. The silence is filled with the very thing you have been trying to avoid. It is filled with the presence you have been trying to ignore. This love, patient as the sunrise and faithful as gravity, has been calling your name since before your birth, waiting for you to pause long enough to hear it.

Some days I forget. Some days the old fog rolls back in, and I find myself moving again— reaching toward something, retreating from something, staying busy because standing still is the hardest thing a restless soul can do. The muscles of escape are overdeveloped. The muscles for standing still have withered from years of disuse.

But the stillness waits. It does not demand. It does not chase. It simply waits for you to stop long enough to remember what you already know.

Stop. Be sober. Look up with the eyes of the heart.

Everything begins here.

I cannot overstate the importance of this beginning. Everything that follows in this book— every chapter, every concept, and every instruction—depends on this single prerequisite. Stop. Be sober. Look up. Without this, nothing else is possible. With this, everything else becomes possible.

The stopping is not passive. It is the most active thing you will ever do. It takes more strength to stand still than to run. It takes more courage to face the silence than to fill it. It takes more willpower to surrender than to fight. The paradox of spiritual awakening is that the first act of power is the admission of powerlessness. The first step forward is the one that stops.

I think of my early days in recovery, sitting in meetings, listening, not understanding half of what I heard but knowing—with the eyes of the heart—that I was in the right place. I did not understand the program. I did not understand the path. I did not understand the God they talked about. But I understood the stopping. I understood the stillness. I understood that for the first time in my adult life, I was sitting still, and the world was not ending.

The silence was not killing me. The truth was not destroying me. It was, in fact, doing the opposite.

It was building something new. Something that could not have been built while I was running. It required stillness, silence, and the willingness to look up.

I think about the difference between hearing and listening. I heard thousands of words before I listened to one. In meetings, in conversations, in the quiet counsel of people who cared about me, the words entered my ears and bounced off something hard inside me. I could repeat what was said. I could nod at the right moments. But the words did not land. They could not land because there was no soft ground in me for them to take root. The ground was paved over with opinion, with certainty, with the concrete shell of a man who already knew everything he needed to know.

Listening requires vulnerability. It requires the admission that you do not already have the answer. It requires the softening of the ground— the breaking up of the pavement, the turning of the soil—so that when the seed falls, it can take root. This is what waking up did for me. It did not give me unfamiliar information. It gave me soft ground. It broke up the concrete of my certainty and exposed the earth underneath— --dark, rich, waiting, hungry for something real to grow in it.

The eyes of the heart are not just for seeing. They are for receiving. And receiving is the thing that intensifies the most. Receiving implies acknowledging one's own need. To receive is to stand with open hands instead of fists. To receive is to say, I have enough, I am enough, and I am willing to let something larger than me fill the space I have been trying to fill myself.

The stopping made that possible. The stillness made that possible.

4

Ye At Least Who Can

If not all of you, at least those of you who have the power.

— CORPUS HERMETICUM VII

Not everyone will hear this.

I do not say that with arrogance. I say it with the grief of someone who has watched people I love stay asleep. Who has stood at the edge and turned around to wave, only to see blank faces staring back? Who has tried to explain the door and been met with the same look Truman's neighbors would have given him if he had told them the sky was painted?

The Hermetic text has a startling admission. It does not address all of humanity. It does not promise universal awakening. It says that if not everyone, at least those among you who have power are included. It narrows the audience. It acknowledges a painful truth. Not everyone can hear. Not everyone will.

I have sat in hospital rooms with people I loved and watched them choose the bottle over their lives. Not once. This was not a dramatic, cinematic moment. However, it happens slowly, persistently, with the quiet determination of a person who has decided, at some level beneath reason that the prison they know is preferable to the freedom they do not. And I have learned that there is nothing I can do about it. I cannot pour my willingness onto another person. I cannot open their eyes to what I see. I cannot drag them through the door. The door must be walked through voluntarily.

My older sister raised me. She cared for me growing up like a second mother, like a guardian. She passed away fighting this stark reality. We were side by side, fleeing family hardships together. The only relief either of us found came from numbing the blood of past trauma. I cried so hard, wishing with all my might that I could save her from the grip of addiction. I went to see her in the hospital as she battled liver cancer. All she could say was, "now you get to experience what an alcoholic death looks like."

She endured undeserved guilt and sadness until the very end. My heart was broken. I said to God, "She is so deserving of this present— I would trade places so she could know what just a moment of happiness feels like." She was smart. She held a prominent position in the corporate world. And none of it saved her. Many do not understand that the source is an internal issue that defies external cures.

This issue is not about intelligence. It is not about merit. It is not about being better or worse than anyone else. It is about something I have come to call willingness—a quality that cannot be manufactured, cannot be argued into existence, and cannot be transferred from one person to another. Either the ground of your soul is ready to receive the seed, or it is not. And there is no shame in either condition. The ground does not choose its season.

But for those who have the power—for those who are reading these lines and feeling something stir, some vibration in the chest, some recognition that these words are landing on prepared soil— this book is for you.

I spent years in the rooms of recovery. I have seen every kind of person walk through those doors. I have seen the desperate individuals who arrive with trembling hands and swollen eyes. The court-ordered individuals sit in the back, their arms crossed, as they count the minutes. Some come because their wives have threatened to leave. Some come because they have woken up in a hospital and are unable to recall the past three days. I have seen a transformation in some of them, akin to a light bulb connecting to a current. Something in them recognizes the truth they are hearing. Something in them has been waiting for exactly this word, spoken at exactly this moment, in exactly this room.

And I have watched others sit in the same room, hear the same words, and leave unchanged. It is not that the words were incorrect. Not because the program was flawed. The ground was not yet prepared. This was because the willingness to change had not yet developed. Because the pain had not yet cut deep enough to crack them open. And I have learned not to judge this. The seed will come when the season comes. It is not my job to force the spring.

Jung wrote about individuation—the process by which a person becomes who they truly are, beneath the masks and roles and inherited identities. He believed this process was not for everyone. This is not due to the unworthiness of some individuals, but rather because the process needs a confrontation with the unconscious, a task for which most people lack the necessary preparation. It requires the dissolution of everything you thought you were. It requires walking into the darkness of your psyche and facing what lives there. It requires sitting with the shadow, the monster, the thing under the bed, and discovering that the thing under the bed is you.

Most people would rather live behind the painted sky. And I do not blame them. It is warm. The scripts are comfortable. The painted sky is beautiful, in its way. Leaving is terrifying. Leaving means giving up every certainty, every identity, and every false comfort that has kept you functional in a dysfunctional world.

I carry this hope with me like a stone in my pocket—smooth from turning, warm from handling. The hope that every soul behind the painted sky is temporary. That every covering has a seam that will eventually give way. The pain, meaningless now, is quietly at work, thinning the fabric, loosening the threads, and laying the groundwork for the moment when everything unravels and the light floods in.

I cannot make that moment happen for anyone else. This is the hardest lesson I have learned in recovery. I cannot force the season. I cannot drag someone through the door. I can stand on the other side and call out. I can extend my hand through the opening. I can write books and speak in meetings and tell my story in every room that has me. But the walking through—that sacred, terrifying, irreducible act of stepping from the known into the unknown— that must be done by the person themselves. No one can be carried through the door. You walk through on your own two feet, or you do not walk through at all.

This is why I have such reverence for the ones who walk. Every person who walks through the door is performing an act of courage that the world will never fully appreciate. The world does not see the door. The world does not know it exists. The world looks at the one recovering and sees someone who stopped doing a harmful thing, which is true but so incomplete as to be almost misleading. What they have done is something far more radical than stopping a behavior. They have left a world. They have walked out of a reality that everyone around them accepts as real, and they have stepped into a territory that has no map, no guarantee, and no safety net.

That takes something that goes beyond courage. It takes the brand of holy desperation that only the broken have. The willingness to lose everything—including the self you have been pretending to be—for the chance at something real.

I bow to every person who has walked through. Broken, shaking, unsure of what lies ahead—they walked. And the angels, the text assures us, are rejoicing.

There is a difference between those who want recovery and those who need it. The need is universal. Every human being is, to some degree, asleep. Every human being is walking through it. But wanting—the active, burning, desperate desire to wake up—that is rare. That is the power the Hermetic text describes. That is the crack through which the light enters.

I believe the word chosen in the title of this book is not about selection. It is about willingness. You are not chosen by some external hand that plucks you from the crowd and says, "You, you are the special one." You are chosen by your willingness to hear. The light finds its way through the crack in your armor. The pain that prevents you from sleeping has chosen you. The desperation that drew you to the rooms, to this page, or to the threshold you stand at now has chosen you.

If you are reading this, something in you is ready. Something in you has the power. I do not know what brought you here—desperation, curiosity, grief, or something you cannot name. But you are here. And the text was written for you. At least for you.

Not everyone will hear.

But you can.

And because you can, you must. That sounds harsh, but I mean it as the greatest kindness I know how to offer. If you have the capacity to wake up, the capacity itself is a calling. It is not an option. It is a responsibility. Not a burden—a gift wrapped in a responsibility. The gift is an awakening. The responsibility is to share it.

I do not know why some people are empowered and others do not. I do not understand why some souls are ready while others are not. I do not pretend to understand the mechanics of grace. But I know this: if you are reading these words and feeling something stir— something deeper than intellectual interest, something more visceral than curiosity—then the ground is ready. The seed is already landing. The season has already turned.

Do not waste the season. Seasons pass. The ground that is ready today may harden tomorrow. The crack that lets the light in today may close. If you do not act, the willingness that led you to this page could diminish. I have seen it happen. I have watched people stand at the threshold of the door, feel the breeze from the other side, and turn back because the familiar was comfortable and the breeze was strange.

Do not turn back. You can hear this. You are hearing it now. That is enough. That is all the power you need.

I want to speak directly to the person who feels unworthy of the calling. The individual who reads these words and believes, "This is not for me," is the target of my message." I have gone too far. I have done too much damage. I have wasted too many years. I have squandered too many chances. It is too thick. The tomb is too deep. The flood has carried me too far from shore.

I know that voice. I listened to it for years. It is the voice making its final argument. It says, "You are not one of the ones who can." You are one of the people who cannot. Stay inside. Stay in the flood. Stay where you belong.

The voice is lying.

If you can feel these words—if there is even a flicker of recognition, even the faintest vibration in the place where the eyes of the heart live—then you are one of the ones who can. The very fact that you have read this far is evidence. The cloak does not allow unready souls to reach this page. The fact that you are here, reading, feeling something stir beneath the concrete of your certainty, means the ground is softer than you think.

There is no minimum qualification for walking through the door. No entrance exam. No background check. The door does not ask where you have been. It only asks if you are willing to step through. And willingness, as I have said and will say again, does not require strength. It requires exhaustion. It requires the moment when the fight has spent its last reserve of resistance and the soul, quiet, patient, and indestructible, finally has room to move.

You are not too far gone. You are exactly far enough. The distance you have traveled into the darkness is the exact distance from which the light will be most astonishing when you turn around.

5

The Ill of Ignorance

The vice of ignorance floods the whole earth and utterly destroys the soul shut up in the body, preventing it from anchoring in the havens of deliverance.

— CORPUS HERMETICUM VII

Ignorance is not what I thought it was.

The world taught me that ignorance meant not knowing things. Not having enough information. Not reading enough books, attending enough lectures, or accumulating enough facts. But I already knew what the Hermetic text meant by ignorance before I ever read it—because I had been living inside it. This was not a lack of education. This was a condition embedded in my being, woven into the fabric of what I was. No amount of data could cure it because it was not an absence of knowledge. It was an absence of awareness. The soul had fallen asleep within itself. I did not need more input. I needed to wake up.

But the ignorance the Hermetic text describes is something entirely different. It is not a lack of knowledge. It is a forgetting. A deep, systemic forgetting of what we are and where we come from and what we are meant for. It is not that we do not have the information. It is that we have forgotten what the information means. We have forgotten the context. We have forgotten the story we are inside of. We are characters in a novel who have forgotten the author, the plot, and the title of the book.

The text calls it a vice. Not a mistake. Not an accident. A vice is a force that grips you, has its own momentum, and pulls you down, holding you there. And it says this vice floods the whole earth. Not just part of it. Not just the uneducated or the unenlightened. The whole earth.

The whole earth. That means the doctor and the sufferer. The priest and the atheist. The philosopher and the man who has never opened a book. The monk in his cell and the executive in his corner office. The therapist and the patient. The teacher and the student. All of them drowning in the same flood. All of them are subject to the same illness. The illness is not personal. It is not individual. It is the condition of being human in a world that has lost its memory.

I find this both devastating and liberating. Devastating because it means there is no safe category, no exempt population, and no island of consciousness surrounded by the flood. Nobody gets a pass. Nobody escapes by virtue of their education or their practice or their goodness. The flood is comprehensive. The ignorance is total. It touches everyone.

But it is also liberating. Because if the disease is universal, then the cure is not reserved for the elite. If everyone is sick, then the medicine is for everyone. The havens of deliverance do not have a guest list. The door in the painted sky does not require a membership card. The light cleansed of darkness shines on everyone who lifts their gaze. The chosen are not chosen by their credentials. They are chosen by their willingness. And willingness does not require a degree, a pedigree, or a bank account. It requires only the desperation or the grace to say yes.

The illness is forgetting.

I forgot who I was. That sounds dramatic, and it is. But I mean it. I forgot that I was more than a body. I forgot that I had a soul—and I do not mean that in a poetic sense. I mean, there is a part of me that existed before this body and will exist after it, a part that is not made of flesh and blood, a part that does not age and cannot be destroyed. I forgot that. The world taught me to forget it. Every institution I passed through—school, work, medicine, entertainment—trained me to identify with the body, the mind, and the personality. The costume. Never the actor underneath. Never the awareness of wearing it.

The text says this ignorance utterly destroys the soul shut up in the body. That phrase haunts me. Shut up in the body. The soul is not comfortably living in the body. It is imprisoned. It is locked inside, and the lock is ignorance itself. We do not know we are prisoners because we have forgotten there is anything outside the cell. We have decorated the cell. We have installed entertainment in the cell. We have made the cell so comfortable that the idea of leaving it sounds insane.

But the soul knows. Even when the mind has forgotten, the soul knows it is trapped. That is the source of the ache. That is the restlessness. That is the unexplainable dissatisfaction that persists even when every material need has been met. The soul, shut up in the body, pounding on walls that nobody can hear, screaming in a frequency that the mind's instruments cannot detect.

Jung described the unconscious as an ocean that the conscious mind floats upon. Most of us live our entire lives on the surface, thinking the surface is all there is. We are driven by currents we cannot see—ancestral patterns, childhood wounds, collective fears, archetypal forces—and we call these currents our choices. But they are not choices. They are the flood. The unconscious overwhelming the conscious. The soul drowning in a body has forgotten how to pilot.

In recovery, they call it a disease. But the disease goes deeper than any single substance or behavior. The recovery tradition makes this plain: These principles—trust God, clean house, help others—apply to the problems of living that confront us all. The disease is the forgetting itself. The entire human race is sick with it. Those in acute suffering are simply the ones whose symptoms became too loud to ignore. Their gift—and it is a terrible, beautiful gift—is that the illness announces itself. It does not hide. It screams. And the screaming, painful as it is, is what drives the sufferer to seek the cure.

The havens of deliverance. That phrase from the text sends a chill through me every time I read it. There are havens. There are safe harbors. There are places where the soul can anchor, rest, and remember what it is. But the flood prevents us from reaching them. We cannot anchor in the havens because we do not know the havens exist. We are so deep in the water that we have forgotten there is land. We are so far from shore that the word "shore" has lost its meaning.

This is what I was. A soul shut up in a body, drowning in a flood I was unaware of the flood and unable to reach a shore I did not know existed. And the most insidious part of the illness was that I felt fine. I felt normal. Everyone around me was drowning too, so I assumed this was simply what breathing looked like.

The cure begins with the diagnosis. You are sick. Not because you are broken, but because you have forgotten. Not because something is missing, but because something has been buried. The soul is still there, shut up in the body, waiting. The havens are still there, beyond the flood, waiting.

The only thing needed is remembering.

Remembering. Not learning. Not achieving. Not accumulating merit or performing rituals or subscribing to the correct theology. Remembering. The word itself holds the cure—remembering, putting back together what was dismembered. The soul was dismembered by the forgetting. It was scattered pieces of it lodged in old wounds, old identities, and old stories. Recovery is remembering gathering the scattered pieces and putting them back together.

I think about the parable of the prodigal son, which is the same story the Hermetic text tells in different language. The son leaves the father's house. He goes into a far country. He squanders his inheritance. He ends up feeding pigs, starving, destitute. And then he remembers. He remembers the father's house. He remembers who he is. He remembers where he came from.

And the remembering is the beginning of the return.

The father does not go looking for him. The father waits. Not passively, but with the active patience of a love that knows the son must choose to return. The door is open. The light is on. The feast is prepared. But the son must turn his face toward home. The son must remember.

This is the story of every sufferer. Every seeker. Every soul behind the painted sky. We have gone into a far country. We have squandered our inheritance. We have forgotten the father's house. And the cure is not punishment, not penance, not the acquisition of something new. The cure is remembering.

I have a practice I want to share, because it connects the Hermetic teaching to the daily experience of recovery in a way that I find essential. Every morning, before the noise of the day begins, I sit in silence, and I ask one question: What have I forgotten?

Not what do I need to learn. Not what should I do today. What have I forgotten?

The question reframes the entire spiritual project. It shifts the orientation from acquisition to recovery—not recovery in the clinical sense, though it is that too, but recovery in the literal sense. Recovering what was lost. Retrieving what was buried. Finding, in the rubble of a life lived under it, the pieces of the soul that were scattered by the forgetting.

Some mornings the answer is immediate. I have forgotten that I am not in charge. I have forgotten that my worth does not depend on my productivity. I have forgotten that the person who annoyed me yesterday is also a soul also trapped, also a prisoner behind a painted sky, also deserving of the same compassion I needed when I was at my worst.

Other mornings the silence just holds the question without answering it. And that is enough. The asking itself is a form of remembering. The willingness to acknowledge that something has been forgotten is the first crack in the amnesia. The soul, hearing the question, stirs. Not with an answer, necessarily. But with the recognition that someone is finally asking.

The Hermetic tradition calls this anamnesis—the un-forgetting. Plato used the same concept. Learning is not the acquisition of new knowledge. It is the remembering of knowledge the soul already owns. The teacher does not fill an empty vessel. The teacher helps the vessel remember what it already holds.

This is what the rooms do at their best. They do not teach you to stop. They help you remember who you are when you are not hiding.

The havens of deliverance are the father's house. The covering of ignorance is the far country. And the moment of remembering—the moment the prodigal looks up and says, "I will go back"—that is the beginning of everything.

I have a theory about why the ones in the deepest pain are so often the ones who find the door. It is not because they are special. It is because they are sick enough to seek the cure. Acute suffering accelerates the universal illness to a pace that cannot be ignored. The person who drinks moderately, who consumes moderately, who sleeps moderately—this person may go an entire lifetime without the illness announcing itself. The symptoms are there—the restlessness, the vague dissatisfaction, the sense that something is missing—but they are quiet enough to be managed. The person manages the symptoms and calls it a life.

The sufferer cannot manage the symptoms. The volume is too loud. The pain is too acute. The forgetting has become so extreme that it has turned against the body itself, and the body is screaming. And in that screaming—in the unbearable volume of the untreated illness—the sufferer is driven to seek what the moderate person never looks for. In desperation, they look for the cure. And the cure, it turns out, is not the treatment of any single disease. The cure is the treatment of the human condition. The sufferer stumbles into the medicine that every human being needs but most are not desperate enough to take.

Even the founders of the recovery movement knew this. They acknowledged that many people who never struggled with a substance have found, through the practice of these principles, a way to meet the other difficulties of life. Regardless of their specific struggle, these principles provide a path to wholeness and purpose. Read that again. Regardless of the struggle. The program that was written for the desperate, for the drowning, for the ones whose illness screamed the loudest— that program turns out to be medicine for the universal condition. And the proof is in the proliferation. There are now over two hundred distinct twelve-step fellowships worldwide. Not just for alcohol. Not just for drugs. For gambling, for eating, for codependency, for debt, for sex, for workaholism, for emotions, for grief, for clutter. Two hundred different names for the same disease. Two hundred doorways into the same room. Because the flood does not discriminate. It drowns the executive in his corner office as surely as it drowns the man on the street. It carries the overachiever as swiftly as the dropout. It pulls under the religious and the secular, the educated and the unschooled, and the young and the old. The symptoms differ. The disease is one. And neither does the cure.

This is what I mean when I say suffering is a terrible, beautiful gift. Terrible because of the suffering. Beautiful because the suffering cracks it open. And through the cracks, the light of remembering enters.

The prodigal's gift was not his virtue. It was his hunger. He had spent everything. He had nothing left. And in the nothing, he remembered the father's house.

6

Gain The Haven

"Surely you will not sink in this great flood? Those of you who can will take the ebb and gain the haven of deliverance and anchor there."

— CORPUS HERMETICUM VII

The flood is everywhere, and it moves in one direction.

I have come to think of it as a current. A great, invisible river that runs through the center of the world, sweeping everything along with it. Culture is this current. Convention is this current. The collective momentum of seven billion people all moving in the same direction without asking where they are going—that is the flood.

And almost everyone is in it.

I was in it for most of my life. I did not know I was in it because the current felt like solid ground. I went to school because everyone went to school. I pursued career goals because that is what you do. I measured my life by the same metrics everyone around me used—money, status, comfort, and security. And none of it felt wrong because the entire world was doing the same thing. The flood does not feel like a flood when you are surrounded by other people drowning.

The text asks a question that stopped me. Surely you will not sink in this great flood. There is urgency in it. Desperation. As if the voice behind these words is standing on the shore, watching people go under, calling out to anyone who will listen. Surely you will not. As if to say, you of all people, you who are reading this, you who have felt the current pulling— surely you will not let it take you.

Taking the ebb. That is the instruction. The ebb is the counter-current, the movement of water back toward shore when the tide goes out. While the flood carries everything outward—into distraction, into materialism, into the ever-expanding noise of the world—the ebb pulls inward. Toward silence. Toward stillness. Toward the shore.

To take the ebb means to swim against the current. It means moving in the opposite direction of the entire world. And this is the hardest thing a person can do because every cell of your social body screams that you are going the wrong way. The crowd is over there. Safety is over there. Normal is over there. And here you are, swimming alone toward a shore no one else seems to see.

Jung understood this. He described the process of individuation as a separation from the collective—not a rejection of humanity, but a willingness to stop being carried by it. The individuating soul must withdraw from the herd instinct that keeps most people unconscious. It must stand apart, face its own shadow, and find its own center. This is not arrogance. It is a necessity. You cannot wake up while you are still being carried along in the sleep of the crowd.

The Bible describes it as the narrow gate. The broad road leads to destruction—not because God punishes, but because the current carries you away from yourself. The narrow road leads to life—not because it is morally superior, but because it runs against the flood.

I came to understand that I did not need someone else's God to begin. My understanding—incomplete, unpolished, barely formed—was enough to take the first step. The moment I admitted that something intelligent lived behind the design of this world, something shifted. A direction appeared where there had been none. And then the truth that broke me open: the Divine does not demand perfection from those who seek it. The door to the Spirit is wide. It does not ask for credentials. It does not turn away the unfinished, the uncertain, or the ones who arrive crawling. It only asks that you come honestly.

When I read those words, I cried so hard. Because I always knew in my heart that God was as loving as those words described. But I had spent my whole life feeling guilty. Feeling not good enough. Trying to perform at a standard of perfection I could never reach. Unable to accept my falls in life as a path to awareness. Instead, the guilt kept the impostor fed on false pride. It was never the shame of not being good enough that held me. It was the refusal to let go. And the letting go was my human right—my right to be human, to be loving, to accept who I had forgotten I was. The shedding of it is the path to remembering.

I remember the moment I understood this. I was newly awake, standing outside a meeting, watching the traffic on the highway.

All those cars, all those people, all moving. Going to work. Going home. Going to the store. Going, going, going. And I thought to myself, "They are all caught in the flood."" And so was I, an hour ago. The only difference between me and them is that I stopped. I reached for the eave.

The haven of deliverance. The text promises it exists. A place to anchor. A place where the flood cannot reach you. I have seen it in prayer, meditation, and the silence between thoughts. It is not a physical location. It is a state of being. A place inside where the soul remembers itself.

A harbor in the storm of the world's noise. And when you find it, even briefly, you understand why the text uses the word "anchor." Because the haven is not a place you visit. It is a place you fasten yourself to. A place you grip with everything you have, because the current will try to pull you back.

I anchor myself through practice. I anchor myself through the daily disciplines of recovery, which include meetings, prayer, meditation, service, inventory, and a relentless commitment to honesty. These are not obligations. They are anchors. They are the ropes that hold me to the haven when the flood surges. Without them, the current would carry me back into the stream. Without them, I would drift, slowly at first, then faster, back into the flood that nearly drowned me.

The haven is not a one-time discovery. It is a daily return. Every morning, I anchor again. Every morning, I reset the ropes. Every morning, I face the current and say, "Not today." Today I stay.

Today I hold. Today I remain fastened to the shore that the flood cannot reach.

Some days the anchoring is easy. The haven is close, the water is calm, and the ropes are strong. Some days the anchoring is a battle. The current is fierce, the ropes strain, the haven feels distant and theoretical, and I wonder if I imagined the whole thing. Those are the days when the practice matters most. Those are the days when the discipline becomes the difference between drowning and standing.

I did not build these disciplines because I am disciplined. I built them because I am desperate. Desperation is the mother of practice. The man who drowned does not need to be convinced to learn to swim.

But you must swim for it. You must take the ebb. And you must keep swimming even when everyone around you thinks you are going the wrong direction.

The flood will not stop. It does not care about you. It is not malicious—it is simply the weight of the collective unconscious, moving as it has always moved, carrying everything along. The question is not whether the flood exists. The question is whether you will sink in it.

Surely you will not.

I think about the flood in its modern form, and I see it most clearly in the tyranny of the screen. The screens are the flood's most efficient delivery system. They carry the current directly into your living room, your bedroom, and your pocket. They ensure that the flood never recedes, that the ebb never arrives, and that the organs of perception are kept in a permanent state of stimulation that masquerades as connection.

I am not a Luddite. I do not believe technology is evil. But the screen is the newest weave of the false skin—a thread so seamlessly woven into modern life that removing it feels like removing a limb. The screen keeps us in the flood the way the bottle kept me in the fog. It provides a constant, low-grade numbing that prevents the waking the text demands. It fills every gap where silence might enter. It blocks every window where the light might come through.

I had to set boundaries with the screen the way I set boundaries with the bottle. Abstinence would be impractical. But discipline. Specific hours when the screen goes dark. Specific practices that reclaim the inner space the screen tries to colonize. A morning hour with no input. An evening hour with no stimulation. Borders drawn around the flood to create a small dry patch where the ebb can find me.

These boundaries are not popular. The world runs on screens. The economy depends on your attention. The entire infrastructure of modern communication assumes your constant availability. Setting limits feels antisocial.

Setting limits feels like withdrawal.

It is withdrawal. It is the same withdrawal. I felt it when I put down the bottle. The same restlessness, the same anxiety, the same desperate urge to reach for the thing that fills the silence. And on the other side of that withdrawal, the same gift: the silence itself, no longer empty but full. Full of the ebb. Full of the current that runs beneath the flood. Full of the quiet, persistent pull toward shore.

The ebb is not just about stopping a behavior. It is about getting out of the current entirely. It is about building a life that moves against the flood, not just a life that removes one ingredient from the flood and keeps everything else. Recovery is not subtraction. It is revolution. It is the total reorientation of your life away from the direction the world is moving and toward the shore the world has forgotten exists.

There is something essential about the ebb itself because it is not intuitive. The ebb is not simply the opposite of the flood. It is not swimming upstream with gritted teeth and white knuckles, fighting the current through sheer willpower. That approach exhausts you. I tried it. I tried to force my way to the shore through determination alone, and the current was stronger than my will. It always is.

The ebb is something different. It is a surrender to a different current—one that flows beneath the flood, invisible, quieter, but more powerful. The mystics called it grace. The recovery tradition calls it a power greater than ourselves. The Hermetic tradition calls it the light cleansed of darkness. Whatever name you give it, the ebb is not something you generate. It is something you allow. You stop fighting the flood, and you let the deeper current carry you. You do not swim to the shore. You are drawn to the shore by something that wants you there more than the flood wants to keep you.

This is the paradox that took me years to understand. Effort is needed—the effort to stop. This effort involves ceasing to struggle, managing, and trying to control the current. The effort is not in the swimming but in the letting go. And letting go, for a person who has spent their entire life gripping, is the hardest work there is.

I have a practice I was taught by an old man in the rooms who had more years of recovery than I had years of living. He told me to start each morning by holding my hands out in front of me, palms up, fingers open. Just that. Just the physical gesture of releasing. And then to say, aloud or silently, "I am not in charge today." Whatever comes, I will not try to control it. Whatever goes, I will not try to hold it. I will let the ebb take me where it takes me.

It sounded like nonsense the first time I heard it. It sounded like the abdication of responsibility. But I tried it because the alternative was drowning. And what I discovered was this: the mornings I opened my hands were the mornings the current shifted. Not because I had manipulated anything. Because I had stopped manipulating everything. The ebb was already there. It had always been there. I just could not feel it while my fists were clenched.

The flood is the default. The ebb is the grace. And the difference between them is the position of your hands.

7

Seek A Guide

*Then, seek a guide to take you by the hand and lead
you to the portals of knowledge.*

— CORPUS HERMETICUM VII

You cannot do this alone.

I tried. Believe me, I tried. I thought I could read my way to awakening. I thought I could think my way through the door. I stacked up books like bricks and tried to build a staircase out of concepts. But concepts are not stairs. They are pictures of stairs. And you cannot climb a picture.

The Hermetic text is direct about this. Seek a guide. Not seek a book. Not seek a philosophy. Not seek a system, a method, or a technique.

Seek a guide—a person, a living human being, to take you by the hand.

That detail matters. Not by the intellect. Not by argument. By the hand. The transmission is personal. It passes from one human being to another through the oldest technology in existence—presence. Touch. The willingness of one soul to walk alongside another through the dark.

In the rooms, we call this person a shepherd. The one who has been where you are going, who walks ahead of you on the path, who turns around and reaches back. Not to carry you. To guide you. This means that I have walked through this part of my life, and I am still standing. Come.

I had a shepherd who saved my life. He did not save it by giving me information. He saved it by being there. By showing up. By telling me the truth when I was lying to myself. By refusing to let me drown in my own thinking. He did not hand me a map. He walked the territory with me.

Jung wrote about this archetype—the wise old man, the guide figure who appears in dreams and myths and at critical junctures in the individuation process. The guide is not the destination. The guide is the one who knows the way because he has walked it himself. He cannot walk it for you, but he can walk it with you.

The portals of knowledge. That is where the guide leads. The guide leads you not to the knowledge itself, as no one can provide you with that. But to the portal, the doorway, the threshold. The guide brings you to the edge of the territory where your own encounter must happen. He can tell you what he saw when he walked through. But you are seeing will be yours.

I think about the men and women who guided me. My shepherd. A counselor who saw through my defenses. A priest who spoke to something in me I did not know existed. An old man in a meeting who said three sentences that rearranged my entire life. None of them were perfect. None of them had all the answers. But each of them had walked ahead of me, and each of them was willing to reach back.

The text says seek. That verb is active. It implies effort. The guide does not come to you while you sit on the couch. You must go looking. You must show up in the rooms, in the churches, in the conversations, and in the places where people who have walked through the door gather. You must be willing to be led, which means giving up the mind's favorite illusion: that it does not need anyone else.

I was a man who needed no one. I was self-sufficient. Self-reliant. Self-made. And every one of those selves was a lie. I was drowning, and I was too proud to reach for the hand being extended to me.

The moment I reached for it was the moment everything began to change.

Seek a guide. Take the hand that is offered. Let yourself be led to a door you cannot yet see.

The portals of knowledge do not open to the proud. They open to the desperate. And desperation, in the economy of the spirit, is a form of grace.

I think about this chain of transmission— the hand-to-hand passage of truth from one awakened soul to another—and I am humbled by it. I did not find the door alone. No one does. The myth of the self-made spiritual seeker is exactly that—a myth. Every person who has walked through the door was led there by someone who walked through before them. And that person was led by someone before them. The chain stretches back through centuries, through the rooms, through Jung's consulting room, through the Hermetic schools of Alexandria, through the mystery traditions of Egypt and Greece, through whatever original moment a human being first looked up from the ground and understood something clearly at last.

I am a link in that chain. So is my shepherd. So is the stranger in a meeting whose few quiet words rearranged my life. So is Jung, writing his letter in 1961 about the spiritual thirst beneath all suffering? And so is the ancient voice behind the Corpus Hermeticum, standing at the edge of the old world, calling out to the drowning: seek a guide.

The guide does not need to be a guru. The guide does not need to be a saint. The guide only needs to have walked the path ahead of you and be willing to turn around. In my experience, the best guides are the ones with the most wreckage—because their wreckage is what cracked them open, and their cracks are where the light comes through.

If you are looking for a guide, look for someone with scars. Look for someone who walks with a limp. Look for someone who does not pretend to have it all figured out but who has a steadiness in their eyes that tells you they have seen something real. That is your guide. Take their hand. Let yourself be led.

I did not pick my shepherd. He was a fellow traveler on the nature path. He found me the way the shepherd in the parable finds the lost sheep. Jesus said, "What man of you, having a hundred sheep, if he has lost one of them, will leave the ninety-nine in the open country and go after the one which is lost until he finds it?" My shepherd was not standing at a podium in a shiny suit, climbing the culture ladder to nothingness. He was at the firing line. The gutter. The place where the dying goes when they have run out of places to run.

I was sinking. I could feel it—the slow pull of a life I could no longer hold together, the weight of every lie and every failure dragging me under. Quicksand stretched in every direction, and every move I made pulled me deeper. I had reached the place where you wish for the end, where the idea of living one more day in the condition you are in is unbearable. And in that place, at the very bottom, with nothing left to bargain with and no one left to perform for, I said the most meaningful prayer I had ever spoken. Three words. Please help me. That was the only willingness I needed.

The true shepherd is not the one who has never been lost. The true shepherd is the one who has been so lost, so deep in the grave, that he is no longer afraid of the dark. The truly recovered are not afraid of hell or the dream any longer. Once you see the truth, you cannot unsee it. The recovered shepherd will jump down into the sufferer's grave and be the light to guide him out. That is the hand the Hermetic text describes. Not a clean hand reaching down from a safe distance. A scarred hand, reaching from inside the pit, because the guide has been there and knows the way.

There is a moment in the relationship between guide and guided that is sacred and rarely talked about. It is the moment of confession. Not the formal ritual of a religious ceremony. It is the raw, unscripted moment when a human being shares with another the complete truth about themselves, including the parts they have never spoken aloud.

When I did my personal inventory, I was already desperate to have God take everything I had been dragging all my life. Every resentment, every fear, and every lie I had told myself and others. I wrote it all down. And then I sat in my shepherd's living room, and I read it aloud to him and to God. Every word. The things I had never said to another human being. The weight I had carried so long it had fused to my bones.

And when I finished, we took what I had written—the pages, the inventory, the years of accumulated darkness. I had refused to release— and we placed them in a brass burner. We lit them. And I watched the fire consume every word. It felt like casting the whole burden into Gehenna, gone forever. The flames took what I could not carry and turned it to ash.

After that ceremony, the angels rejoice. I had heard the scripture a hundred times—that heaven celebrates when one lost soul finds its way home. But in that moment, sitting in the quiet of my shepherd's living room with the smell of smoke still in the air, I felt it. For once I felt grace, purpose, and proximity to my higher power. It was a true offering—all of me, laid on the altar, held back nothing. Like the story of Abel, whose offering found favor because it came from the firstborn of his flock, from the best of what he had. I felt favor. I felt love. The dark fog that cleared was the deceiver within—my Cain, the part of me that had killed every good impulse, envied every honest man, and built its identity on resentment and self-will. The sunlight of the spirit shone through me like light through a hologram, pouring out from every wound, every crack, every place I had been broken.

That is the guide. Not someone who has transcended the human condition. Someone who has walked through the worst of it and survived. Someone whose survival is the proof that the path does not end in the darkness. Someone who can sit with your worst and not flinch, because they have already sat with their own.

This is how the chain works. Not through books. Not through doctrines. Through the living transmission from one awakened soul to another.

The guide does not hand you a manual. The guide hands you a piece of themselves—the piece that was forged in the fire, the piece that survived the flood, the unbreakable piece because it has already been broken.

And you carry that piece with you. And one day, when someone else is sitting in the ash of their old life with nothing left, you hand it to them.

8

Where Shines Clear Light

*"There shines a light cleansed of darkness. There, no
one is drunk. All are sober and they gaze with the
heart toward one who wishes to be seen."*

— CORPUS HERMETICUM VII

A place exists where the fog completely dissipates.

I did not believe this perspective when I first began my journey. I
thought clarity was a spectrum—that you could get a little less
foggy, a little more aware, but the haze would always be there. That
was the best I hoped for. A manageable fog. A functioning unconsciousness.

Recovery as damage control.

But the text describes something else. It describes a place where
the light is cleansed of darkness. Not dim. Not mixed. Cleansed.
A light with no shadow in it. The awakening was so profound that
the word itself could not adequately describe it.

I have been to this place. Not permanently. Not for long. But I
have stood in it, and I can tell you it is real. It happened first in a

moment of prayer that went deeper than I intended. I was not praying for anything—I had run out of requests. I was just sitting with the silence, and it opened. The silence unfolded as if a door had suddenly opened. Like a sky opens. It was as if the dome parted, and it dawned on you that there had been weather above it all along.

In that moment, I was not drunk. Not on anything. I was free from alcohol, self-pity, ambition, and fear. I was simply present. And there was light—not the light you see with your eyes, but the light you see with your understanding. Everything was illuminated. This illumination did not occur in a spectacular vision filled with angels and trumpets. In a quiet knowing. A settling. It felt as though all the fragments of my identity came together at once, allowing me to perceive the shape of the room I was standing in for the first time.

The text says there is no one drunk. I take this to mean that there is a level of consciousness that intoxicants cannot reach. Distractions, fears, cravings, and the endless narration of the chattering mind cannot penetrate this level of consciousness. It is like stepping into an altitude where the air is too thin for the old thoughts to survive. They fall away. And what remains is you—the real you, the one who existed before the fog, the bottle, and the painted sky.

All are sober, and they gaze with the heart. This is what I call the fellowship of the awake. Not a formal group. Not an organization. A recognition. When you meet someone who has been to this place—who has stood in the clean light even once—you know it. Not because they tell you. You can tell because there is a distinct difference in their eyes. Something in the way they hold silence. Their steady presence conveys a sense of having seen the other side.

The text says they gaze toward one who wishes to be seen. That phrase broke something open in me. God wishes to be seen. Not demands. Not commands. Wishes. There is a longing in the Divine that mirrors the longing in us. We ache for God, and God aches for us. The separation is mutual suffering. The reunion is mutual joy.

Jung called this the realization of the Self—the moment when it dissolves enough for the deeper center to emerge. He said it was the goal of the entire individuation process. This transcends happiness, success, or even peace. The Self. The total is you. The Self has always been present, hidden beneath the costumes, complexes, and decades of forgetting.

There is a deeper plane of existence that most people never access. I always thought that was hyperbole. It is not. There is a way of living that runs on a level most people do not know exists. It is not about having experiences. It is about being awake. It is not about what you see. It is about seeing itself.

This is what I have been calling The Chosen Anonymous—a continuation of the recovery of the self-forgetting. Recovery brought me to the door. The clean light is what waits on the other side.

And it is there. It is real. It is waiting for anyone willing to gaze with the heart.

I want to leave this chapter with an invitation that is also a warning. The clean light, once met, creates a responsibility. You cannot stand in the light and then pretend you have never seen it. You cannot visit the haven and then deny it exists. You cannot look at someone who wants to be seen and then say you saw nothing.

The light creates an obligation—not a burden, but a calling. The first obligation is to love yourself as your own best friend. Not in the shallow way the world talks about self-love, but in the way the light demands it—to stop punishing yourself for being human, to stop withholding from yourself the same grace you would offer a stranger. From this love, you should live, make decisions, and treat others based on what you now know to be true. The light is real. It is not a metaphor. It is not a hope. It is the most real thing you have ever encountered.   And once you know that every choice becomes a choice between the light and the costume, between the truth and the lie, between the clean air beyond the walls and the recycled air within.

Some days I choose poorly. Some days, the old way feels more comfortable than the light. Some days the old world feels safer than the sky. But I know now what I am choosing. And that knowledge—the knowledge that I have a choice, that the light exists, that the disguise is not my skin—makes all the difference.

Something shifts when you have been to this place. It is not that the world becomes different. The world stays exactly as it was— broken, beautiful, chaotic, and full of suffering and wonder in equal measure. And that is the revelation. The world does not need to change. You do not need to change it. What happens does not change at all. It is acceptance. Acceptance that you have been living from a self-centered perspective—judging, managing, criticizing, and insisting that everything and everyone conform to your design. And the perspective of the chosen is the opposite of that. It is the memory of a place of self-love so deep and universal that it extends to everything it touches. Acceptance was not passive—it was the most powerful act I had ever committed. Nothing in this life arrives without reason. When I finally understood that something in me released. It was never the world's imperfection. It was my refusal to accept it.

Colors are brighter when you accept them as they are. Not metaphorically. Brighter. Sound is deeper. The taste of food is more vivid. The presence of another person is more tangible. Not because something has been added, but because something has been surrendered—the mind's insistence that everything be other than what it is. For years I appointed myself the judge of everything—every person, every situation, and myself most of all. I could find the fracture in anything. Acceptance dismantled that courtroom. It showed me that every soul has a right to be here, that I do not know what is best for my own life, and that if I cannot see clearly for myself, I have no business prescribing vision for anyone else. The world never needed my correction. It needed my surrender. And in accepting it, I remembered the love that was there all along.

This is the deeper plane. It is not a place you go. It is a way you perceive. It is the quality of consciousness that appears when the wrapping has been removed, the organs of perception have been unblocked, and the heart is open and receiving. It is life lived at full resolution, without the compression and distortion that it imposes.

Because it can only perceive from one point of view—its own. Self-centered to its core, the false self looks at the whole of creation and sees only what threatens it or serves it. I was programmed into this belief by life itself— by parents running from their own egos, by institutions built on self-interest, and by a culture that teaches you to measure and compare and compete before it teaches you to breathe. This delusion is the disease of perception that floods the whole earth. It is not that we cannot see. It is that we see from only one angle, without open-mindedness, without willingness, and without the humility to admit we might be looking at the wrong thing entirely.

I neglected the full picture of gratitude for years. I was focused on the one percent instead of the whole. I was the man who walked into a forest—thousands of trees alive and reaching toward the sky—and fixed his gaze on the single dead one. That dead tree became my entire reality. I built my identity around it. I complained about it. I resented it. And the living forest—the overwhelming evidence of beauty, abundance, and grace—stands all around me, unseen. The deeper plane is what happens when you finally lift your eyes from the dead tree and take in the forest.

I cannot stay there permanently. I wish I could. But I visit increasingly often. And each visit leaves a residue—a trace of the clean light that lingers even after the fog rolls back in. The visits are cumulative. The light builds. The seeing deepens. And gradually, slowly, the default state of consciousness begins to shift from fog to clarity, from sleep to waking, and from darkness to open sky.

And then there is joy, because it is the thing that surprised me most about the clean light. I expected peace. I expected understanding. I expected some form of quiet contentment. What I did not expect was joy—wild, unreasonable, disproportionate joy. Joy that had no external cause. The joy materialized unexpectedly and transformed ordinary moments. Standing in line at the grocery store, I suddenly felt a wave of gratitude so intense that it brought tears to my eyes. Watching the light move across a wall and feeling that the light was alive, that it was seeing me as much as I was seeing it. Sitting quietly with someone and feeling the space between us fill with love.

This delight is not the pleasure the Hermetic text warns against. This is not the loathsome pleasure that stuffs and numbs. This is the natural state of the uncovered soul—the joy that exists beneath it, the delight that was always there but could not be felt through the layers of ignorance. It is not something you achieve. It is something you uncover. It is the soul's native temperature, revealed when the insulation is removed.

I was promised a life beyond anything I could have imagined. I thought that was an exaggeration. It is not. The life beyond is not incrementally better than the life within it. It is categorically different. It runs on different principles. It is powered by a different source. The life within the fiction is powered by will— by effort, by striving, by the exhausting engine of self-reliance. The life beyond is powered by grace—by surrender, by receptivity, by the astonishing discovery that when you stop trying to hold the world together, it holds itself. It also carries you along with it.

The essence of spiritual experience is the awareness of a power greater than ourselves. Some call it God-consciousness. Not God-belief. Not the God theory. Consciousness. It is a direct awareness that is not mediated by doctrine or argument.

The path does not require a specific theology. It requires three things: willingness, honesty, and the humility to remain open. Without these, nothing moves. And the greatest obstacle to awakening is not ignorance—it is the refusal to look. The person who dismisses what they have not examined has built an impenetrable wall of falsehood.

To be open-minded to all spiritual concepts is a humble way of saying, "Stay on the path." The roots grow deeper, and the branches stretch farther. The clean light does not belong to any one tradition, any one theology, or any one set of rooms. It belongs to anyone willing to look up.

When you become the observer—when you step back from the constant noise of the mind and simply watch—you are no longer the self-appointed director trying to control every scene. You are no longer rewriting the script, adjusting the lighting, or insisting that every moment bend to your will. You transform into a completely different entity. You become the watcher of your mind. And the watcher does not perform. The watcher does not react. The watcher simply sees.

This act of observation is what changes everything. When you become an observer of your thoughts instead of obeying them, you become the gatekeeper. A thought arrives—fear, resentment, the old impulse to defend or attack or control— and instead of acting on it, you watch it. You let it pass. You do not chase it. You do not feed it. You keep the keys to your mouth, your fists, and your life. You stand at the gate, and you let the thought walk by like a stranger on the street. It came. It will go. You do not have to follow it home.

The ego lives in the center. The observer stands outside it. And from that vantage point, what the mystics call God-consciousness becomes not a theological abstraction but a lived experience. You see yourself from a distance. You see others with clarity. You see the world as it is, not as the narrator has been narrating it. The impulse to react is replaced by the freedom to respond—or to not respond at all. And in that freedom, you find yourself who you did not know was there. There was a self that existed beyond the noise. It was a self that consistently embodied the stillness beneath the noise. It was a self that consistently embodied the stillness beneath the noise.

I do not live in the clean light permanently.

But I live closer to it than I ever thought possible. And the distance between where I stand and where the light shines grow shorter with every practice, every prayer, every act of surrender, and every moment of presence reclaimed from the greedy hands of it.

I want to be clear about something. I am not writing this from a mountaintop. I am writing this from the path—the same path you are on, with the same rocks underfoot and the same fog rolling in and out. I am not more holy than you. I am not further along than you. I still have the duality to contend with every single day. The pretender does not retire. It does not take a vacation. It wakes up when I wake up, and some mornings it speaks before I do. I still get selfish. I still get afraid. I still catch myself reaching for the old patterns because the old way is familiar, and the light, even now, can feel like too much.

But I am grateful even for that. Thank you to it for creating the contrast. Without the darkness, I would not recognize light. Without it I would not know what it means to stand uncovered. The duality is not a punishment. It is the classroom. And I am still a student.

I write these words not for myself but for love. From a true, bone-deep love for the human condition—for its messiness, its beauty, and its stubborn refusal to be simple. I write because I have been in the flood, and I have been pulled to shore, and the only thing I know how to do with that experience is to reach my hand back into the water. Not as someone who has arrived. I continue to journey towards my destination.

Every day. One breath at a time.

9

No Ear Can Hear Him

"Who is neither heard nor spoken of who is seen not with the eyes but with the mind and heart."

— CORPUS HERMETICUM VII

The deepest things cannot be said.

I have tried. In meetings, in conversations, in the middle of the night when something opens inside me and I want to grab the person next to me and say, "Do you see this?" Do you feel this? I have tried to describe the moment the fog lifts and the light comes through. And every time, the words fall short. This is not due to a lack of words in my vocabulary. Because the thing itself lives beyond the reach of language.

The Hermetic text names the subject directly. People do not hear or speak of God. He is seen not with the eyes but with the mind and heart. This definition is not a limitation. It is a description of the territory. The deepest reality runs on a frequency that the ordinary senses cannot detect. You cannot hear God the way you hear a voice. You cannot see God the way you see a face. The organs of perception that reach the Divine are internal, invisible, and atrophied from disuse.

This perception is clear to those who walk this path. But because it does not run on the familiar frequencies of humanity, it can feel deeply confusing. The words cannot be expressed in a way that human comprehension easily receives. It is the less-traveled path, which some may mistake for solitude. It can be labeled as something broken. The world does not have a category for the person whose inner instruments have come alive, so it reaches for the categories it does have—unstable, oversensitive, delusional. And many who walk this path have internalized those labels, believing something is wrong with them when in fact something is finally right.

Because of this frequency, your senses are heightened. Your sensitivity to vibration increases. You walk into a room, and you can feel the energy before a word is spoken. You sit across from someone, and you can see through the mask of their deception—not because you are judging them, but because it has become transparent to you. The world will tell you that you are too sensitive. That is it talking. This is not oversensitivity. This sensitivity is awareness. And awareness, when honored and not silenced, becomes intuition—the voice of the soul speaking in a language the false self was never taught to hear.

This is why mystics through every tradition have resorted to silence. This is not because they lacked anything to express, but rather because their words could not adequately convey their meaning. Words are containers, and the Divine is not contained. Every sentence about God is a reduction. Every theology is a map that is smaller than the territory.

I understood these concepts for the first time during a period of deep silence. I had taken a week away from everything—no phone, no people, no meetings, no noise. It was just me, the silence, and whatever inhabited it. And on about the third day, something shifted. The silence was no longer empty. It was full. It was filled with an indescribable presence that lacked a name. I was not hearing it. I was not seeing it. I knew it the way you know you are alive—not because someone told you, but because the fact of it is undeniable.

Jung called this the numinous—the experience of the holy that is beyond rational comprehension. He said it was the basis of all true religious experience and could not be made, argued, or taught. You either met it or you missed it. And the encounter always left you changed.

The knowing came from inside, not from outside. No book could give it to me. No teacher could hand it over. The path could point me toward the door, but the realization—the actual seeing—was mine and mine alone. It happened in the privacy of my own inner life, in the silence between the words.

I am a truck driver. Not a theologian. Not a monk. I am a truck driver who drives through the night, covering five hundred miles at a stretch, while practicing meditation in the silence of the cab. I do not turn the music on. I do not fill the darkness with noise. I sit in the silence, and I meditate to the hum of the engine and the road beneath me. My cab must look like a bright light moving through the desert—a single point of illumination crossing miles of nothing. And in that nothing, the wisdom flows. It flows in a way no human voice can speak. It arrives whole, without effort, without invitation, as if it has been waiting for exactly this silence to pour itself into.

I see falling stars on those drives. Not occasionally. Regularly. And every time one streaks across the windshield, I take notice of the moment. I am here. I am awake. I am alone with Oneness—or I am crazy. Those are the only two options, and I have made my choice. I know the clarity that really, truly, all there ever was the One. One God. One Mind. Nothing else truly exists. The separation was the illusion. It was the distance. And in the silence of a truck cab crossing the desert at two in the morning, the distance disappears.

I think this is why so many people never find what they are looking for. They are searching for God using the wrong tools. They are trying to hear God with ears designed for sound. They are trying to see God with eyes designed for light. But God is not sound, and God is not light—not the kind that ears and eyes can catch. God is the awareness underneath sound and light. God is the knowing before thought. God is the silence that holds all noise inside it.

Hidden knowledge is not hidden. That is something I came to understand slowly. The secret is not locked away in some vault. It is not kept from us by some conspiracy of priests or gatekeepers. It is hidden only in the sense that it is not accessible through ordinary means. It is hidden the way the sun is hidden from a man who will not open his eyes. The sun is not hiding. The man is not looking.

And so, I have stopped trying to explain it. I have stopped trying to put into words what words cannot carry. Instead, I point. I point the way someone pointed for me—not at the thing itself, but at the door behind which the thing waits. I say, go in. Be still. Listen with the part of you that has no ears.

You will hear what you must hear.

I want to add that silence is what most people fear most. We are a civilization terrified of silence. We fill every gap with sound. We sleep with the television on. We eat with podcasts playing. We drive with music blasting. We sit in waiting rooms scrolling through content. We want to avoid the silence, but it is the only place we can find what we need.

The silence does not come naturally to the modern mind. You must cultivate it the way you would cultivate a garden—clearing the weeds, preparing the soil, watering, and waiting.

The mind will resist. Something in you will rise. Your entire nervous system, trained by years of constant stimulation, will resist. It is all one thing—the plot. The very fact that the silence feels unbearable is evidence of how badly you need it.

I practice silence now the way I practice waking up—daily, deliberately, as naturally as breathing. But I will tell you something that surprises people. I am not afraid of the silence. I crave it. I crave it the way a man in the desert craves nourishing water. What the world calls loneliness has become oneness. The most complete place I have ever met is what the world considers empty. I avoid noise now. I avoid busyness. I default to the simple road, the quiet road, the one most people pass by because it looks like nothing is there. But everything is there.

When you taste the peace of the silence, you will want more of it. It is not something you have to force yourself to return to. It calls you back. And as you return, something begins to happen. You become a haven yourself—like a lighthouse, steady and bright, not affected by the rough seas of the flood. The wave's crash. The storms rage. And you stand there, lit from within, unmoved. You become your own inner sanctuary. The unknown, which once terrified you, becomes the most comfortable place you have ever been—because inside the unknown lives the knowing. And the knowledge is enough.

Not in words. Not in language. In knowing. In presence. In the unmistakable sense that you are never alone, that you were always connected, that the silence itself is alive, aware, and looking back at you with something that can only be called love.

The difference between knowledge and knowing deserves its attention, because the confusion between these two things has caused more spiritual damage than almost any other misunderstanding.

Knowledge is what the mind collects. It is information, data, facts, theories, and systems of thought. You can acquire knowledge from books. You can test it with logic. You can store it in memory and retrieve it at will. Knowledge is the mind's currency, and the mind is excellent at accumulating it.

However, knowing is a completely different matter. Knowing is what the heart recognizes. It is not collected—it is encountered. It is not tested with logic—it is tested with experience. It is not stored in memory—it is inscribed in the bones. You cannot learn your way to knowledge. You can only live your way to it.

I accumulated knowledge for years. I read everything I could find about spirituality, recovery, psychology, and mysticism. I could discuss the Hermetic tradition with fluency. I could explain the Jungian archetypes with precision. I could recite recovery literature from memory. And none of it changed me. Not one degree. Knowledge without understanding is like furnishing an empty house. It fills the space, but it does not warm it.

The knowing came later, and it came from a direction I did not expect. It came from pain. It came from surrender. It came from the moments when I had no more concepts to hide behind and had to stand naked in the reality of my experience. The knowing came when I stopped reading about the door and walked through it. I ceased my study of the map and began exploring the unfamiliar territory. The turning point occurred when I ceased to analyze the silence and instead began to sit in it.

Jung distinguished between knowing about the unconscious and knowing the unconscious. The first is academic. The second is transformative. You can study dreams for thirty years without experiencing any change. Or you can have one dream that rewrites the architecture of your psyche. The difference is not in the content. It is the mode of encounter. The first is observation. The second is participation. The first keeps you safely on the shore. The second takes you to the water.

The Hermetic text says God is seen not with the eyes but with the mind and heart. The type of seeing described in the text is not a passive reception of visual data. It is the active engagement of the whole being—mind and heart together, intellect and intuition fused, and the thinker and the feeler united in a single act of feeling that transcends both.

This approach is what the rooms of recovery offer at their best. The rooms of recovery offer more than just knowledge about specific diseases. These rooms offer more than just theories about specific conditions. It is the direct encounter with truth in the living, breathing testimony of another human being who has been where you have been and walked through to the other side. That encounter is not information. It is knowing. And knowing, once it takes root, it cannot be uprooted. It becomes part of you. It becomes the new ground on which everything else is built.

10

Tear Off The Cloak

"But first you must rip off the tunic that you wear, the garment of ignorance, the foundation of vice, and the bonds of corruption."

— CORPUS HERMETICUM VII

But first.

Those two words are a warning. They tell you that before the light, before the clean seeing, before the encounter with the Divine—there is something you must do. And the thing is not gentle. The text does not say "remove." It does not say "let go of." It says "rip-off."

This is violence. Sacred violence. The destruction of something that has been covering you so long you have mistaken it for skin.

The tunic. The mask of ignorance. The foundation of vice. The bonds of corruption. The text stacks these names on top of each other like layers, and each layer goes deeper. It is not one thing you must remove. It is everything you have wrapped yourself in since the day you forgot who you were.

In recovery, they call it the personal inventory. You sit down, and you write out everything—every resentment, every fear, every lie, every harm. You lay it all on the table and look at it. None of it. All of it. The instruction is to be fearless and thorough, and those words exist because they have the potential to discourage you from stopping short.

I remember doing my first inventory. I sat at my kitchen table with a legal pad and a cup of coffee, and I began to write. And the first hour was manageable—the surface resentments, the obvious wrongs, and the things I could admit to without losing my sense of self. But then the writing went deeper. Into the places I did not want to go. The writing delved into my past actions, which I had never showed to anyone. I found myself immersed in patterns so ancient that they resembled my own organs. And I wanted to stop. Every cell in my body wanted to stop.

But my guide had told me to keep writing. And so, I did.

That was the ripping. Not a dramatic, cinematic moment. A slow, painful tearing of fabric that had been stitched into my flesh for decades. Every line I wrote was a thread pulled. Every truth I put on paper was a layer removed. And underneath, raw and exposed, was something I did not recognize.

Jung called this shadow work. The shadow is everything about yourself that you have denied, repressed, or hidden from view. It is not just your sins—it is your power, your truth, your unlived life. The shadow holds both your best and worst, and you cannot reach one without facing the other.

The garment of ignorance is woven from the shadow. Every thread is a denial. Every stitch is a moment when you chose not to look. And the tunic grows thicker with each refusal until it becomes your entire wardrobe, your armor, your identity. You walk around wearing your ignorance like a suit and calling it your personality.

In its truest sense, ignorance is not the lack of knowledge. Ignorance is the act of knowing something is wrong yet choosing to do it anyway. It is the gap between what the heart knows and what the hands do. The Bible names this category with devastating precision. James 4:17 says, "*If anyone knows the good, they ought to do and does not do it, it is sin for them.*" This does not refer to ignorance in the sense of simply not knowing.

This is not ignorance in the sense of knowing something and choosing not to act on it. The knowledge is there. The accountability is there. And choosing not to act on what you already know—that is the thickest thread in it.

This book is not about the imperfection of being human. We will fall. We will forget. We will reach for the old patterns out of habit, exhaustion, and fear. That is the human condition, and there is grace for it. But this is about remembering what the heart already knows—and choosing to act on it anyway. Falsehood cannot co-exist with truth. They cannot occupy the same space. Every time you act upon what you know to be true, the veil becomes thinner. Every moment you refuse what the heart is telling you, it thickens. The ripping is not a single act of courage. It involves making a thousand small choices to honor what you already know.

Ripping it off is not a one-time event. I wish it were. I wish I could tell you that I did my personal inventory, the tunic came off, and I stood in the clean light forever. But the truth is that it regrows. Ego is a tireless tailor. It stitches new layers as fast as you tear them away. The ripping is a practice. A daily practice. It is a lifetime commitment to the uncomfortable art of uncovering.

But first. Before the light. Before the seeing. The encounter with the Divine must come before anything else.

You must rip off what covers you.

There is no shortcut through this. There is no detour around it. The caterpillar must dissolve before it can fly.

I want to stay with the caterpillar for a moment, because the metaphor is more precise than most people realize. When a caterpillar enters the chrysalis, it does not simply grow wings. It dissolves. Its entire structure liquefies.

It becomes a formless soup of cells, unrecognizable as the creature it was. And from that dissolution—from that destruction of the old form—the butterfly emerges. Not as a modified caterpillar. The butterfly appears as an entirely new creature.

But here is the part no one talks about. Not all caterpillars survive the transformation. Science tells us that metamorphosis is a high-risk, energy-intensive process that kills many larvae. They die from insufficient strength, from disease, from predators, or from a failure to properly complete what they started. The chrysalis is not a guarantee. It is a gamble. And many do not make it through.

This is what the Hermetic text was telling us from the beginning. At least those of you who have the power will survive, if not all of you.

Not everyone survives the dissolution. Not everyone has the strength to endure the formlessness, the terror of losing everything you thought you were, the long dark in which nothing is recognizable, and the wings that have not yet formed. The text does not say this to discourage. It conveys this message to honor the significance of what is being asked. The transformation is real. The cost is real. And the ones who make it through—the ones who endure the chrysalis and emerge with wings—they are the chosen. Not chosen because they were selected. Chosen because they survived.

The personal inventory is the chrysalis. The writing is the dissolving. And the thing that appears on the other side is not a better version of the old self. It is not an upgrade or a renovation. The old self does not survive. It dies. And from that death, something is reborn. Something is resurrected. A self that could not have existed without the destruction of the old one—the way the butterfly could not exist without the death of the caterpillar.

I have walked with men through this process, and I have watched them resist the dissolution the same way I resisted it. They start strong. They write the easy things—the surface resentments, the obvious flaws in their nature, and the sins that are socially acceptable to admit. Then they meet a significant obstacle. The writing goes deeper, and it screams, and the pen stops. They call me and say they cannot continue. They say it is too much. They say they are afraid of what they will find if they keep digging.

I tell them what my shepherd told me. Keep writing. Not because it will be easy. Because it is necessary. The chrysalis is not optional. The dissolution is not optional. The only shortcut around the inventory is the one that leads back to the bottle.

Saint Francis of Assisi understood the chrysalis. His prayer is the most complete map of this resurrection I have ever read. It does not describe a man asking to be fixed. It describes a man asking to die and be reborn. Where there is hatred, let me sow love. Where there is injury, pardon. Where uncertainty reigns, trust reigns. Where there is despair, hope. Where there is darkness, there is light. Where there is sadness, there is joy. Read the pattern. Every line begins with the old self—the self that hated, that injured, that doubted, that despaired—and asks for its opposite. Not its improvement. It is a replacement. The prayer is a blueprint for rebirth.

And then Francis goes deeper. Grant that I may not so much seek to be consoled as to console, to be understood as to understand, or to be loved as to love. This statement is the end of resistance in simple terms. The old self sought comfort, sought validation, and looked to be filled from the outside. The resurrected self gives. It is in giving that we receive. It is in pardoning that we are pardoned. And it is in dying that we are born to eternal life. The final line encapsulates the essence of the chrysalis. The caterpillar fears the chrysalis only until it learns that flight, not death, awaits. And the soul that has passed through the dissolution of the personal inventory no longer fears death, because it has already died to everything that was not real. What remains after the burning, after the ripping, after the dissolution, is the thing that cannot be destroyed.

And the knowledge of that indestructibility is what the mystics call eternal life. After this knowing, fear dissolves.

Buried in every human being is an awareness of the Divine. Not a learned belief. Not

a theological position. An awareness— embedded in the structure of human consciousness this awareness is like how the blueprint of the butterfly is embedded in the cells of the caterpillar. It is there before the chrysalis. It is there during the dissolution. And it is there, fully realized, when the wings unfold.

The text describes another dimension to the ripping, which I want to name because it is rarely discussed in recovery literature.

The garment is not only personal. It is collective. We are not just wearing our ignorance. We are wearing the ignorance of our families, our cultures, and our civilizations. The patterns that bind us are not all the ones we created. Many of them were inherited— passed down through generations of unconscious living, stitched into it before we were born.

I discovered this item in my inventory. I was writing about my father, about his anger, and about the way his rage had shaped my childhood.

And as I wrote, I realized I was not just writing about him. I was writing about his father. And his father's father. I was uncovering a thread in the false skin that stretched back through generations—a thread of unprocessed pain, of unspoken grief, of violence that had been passed from hand to hand like a poisoned heirloom.

Jung called this area the collective unconscious. The layer of the psyche that belongs not to the individual but to the species. The patterns that live in this layer—the archetypes, the inherited wounds, the ancestral shadows—are not personal. They are human. When you start to pull it off, you find that some threads were sewn by someone else.

Such a discovery does not absolve you of responsibility. It deepens it. The shroud you are peeling off is not solely your own. It is the wrapping of everyone who came before you and could not remove it themselves. When you do the inventory, you are not just healing yourself. You are healing a lineage. You are breaking a chain of unconsciousness that may stretch back centuries. You are doing for your ancestors what they could not do for themselves.

I think about this when the work feels unbearable. When the chrysalis is darkest, I remind myself that I am not doing this for me alone. I am doing it for the man my father could not become because no one showed him the way. I am doing this for the grandfather I have never met, who drowned himself in a country I have never visited. I do it for my future kids, who will inherit something thinner because I had the courage to pull some threads.

The ripping is personal, and it is universal. The veil is yours, and it is everyone's. And every thread you pull makes the fabric lighter for the next person who must wear it.

But first. Before all of this. This is the time before the light, the healing, and the unburdening of the ancestral chain.

You must sit down with the legal pad. You must pick up the pen. You must begin to write.

And you must not stop until it is in pieces at your feet.

11

The Web of Ignorance

"The dark cage, the living death, the sentient corpse."

— CORPUS HERMETICUM VII

The Hermetic text gives three names for the same condition, and each one is more disturbing than the last.

The dark cage. I know what that feels like. I lived in it for years. It is the experience of being enclosed—of moving through the world inside a container you cannot see but can always feel. The cage is not made of iron bars. It is made of perception. It is the narrowing of awareness until the only reality you can access is the small, dark box of your own thinking. You live inside your thoughts. You pace the walls of your mind. And you cannot see that there is an entire universe outside the cage because the cage is all you have ever known.

The living death. That is the condition of a person who is biologically alive but spiritually dead. The body breathes, the heart pumps, and the neurons fire. But the thing that is supposed to animate the body—the soul, the spirit, the spark—is dormant. Locked away. The lights are on, but no one is home. I walked through years of my life in this state. I functioned. I worked. I spoke and ate and slept and laughed. But there was a deadness at the center of it, a hollowness that no amount of activity could fill.

The sentient corpse. This is the most unsettling name because it adds awareness to the deadness. A corpse feels nothing. But a sentient corpse is aware of its own death. It knows something is wrong. It can feel the absence of life without being able to name it. This phenomenon is the condition of anyone who has not yet hit bottom, the depressive who senses the void but cannot find it, and the successful person who has everything and feels nothing. Sentient. Aware. And dead.

Jung described the persona as a mask that we wear so long we forget we are wearing it. The persona is not who you are. It is who you have been trained to be. It is the performance the world demanded, and you delivered it so convincingly that you lost track of the actor underneath. It is a walking corpse dressed in the clothes of the living. It moves through the world with all the appearances of life, but it is not alive. It is animated by habit, by expectation, and by the mechanical repetition of patterns that were installed in childhood and never examined.

In the rooms, they call it being dry but not awake. A person who has stopped the behavior but has not woken up. The substance is gone, but the cage remains. The death is still operative. The corpse is still walking.

Recovery without spiritual awakening is just another form of living.

Death—a polished prison, a well-dressed burial, but the soul still suffocating underneath.

I was dry but not awake for longer than I care to admit. I put down the bottle, and I picked up control. I stopped one form of numbing and started another—productivity. I replaced one cage with another and called it progress. And the whole time, I could feel it—the sentience of the corpse, the awareness of my own deadness, the knowledge that I was walking around in a body but not truly living in it.

There is no halfway position with this disease. You either pick up the instruments of awakening laid at your feet and walk through the door, or you stay in the illusion of the false sky and drown in the flood. There is no third option. There is no comfortable position between awake and asleep. You are moving toward the light, or you are being carried by the current. And the current does not pause.

I am willing to be honest in this book about myself because the truth may save just one person. Two years into recovery, I was drowning. Not in the symptom—in the untreated disease underneath it. My wife was so worried about my life she could barely sleep. I was sober, but I was dying. This is where the spiritual allies need to come together, because the last thing it wants to do is admit defeat. It will let you die before it lets you ask for help. But somewhere inside me there was still a little strength. A little hope. A flicker that had not yet gone out.

Again, I stopped. I was silent. I was listening. And I trusted the cry of my spiritual allies to get help. Humbly, I admitted myself into a clinic because I was suicidal. I say that plainly because it needs to be said plainly. This suffering is very real. Many carry it today homeless on busy city streets, invisible to the people walking past them, drowning in the flood while the world steps over their bodies. I listened to my loved ones. I listened to my doctors. I listened to my heart. The cry is loud, but the surrender is what saves you.

The web of ignorance is not just one prison. It is prisons inside prisons. You escape one cage and find yourself in another. You survive one death and discover you are still not alive. This is why the path of awakening is not a straight line. It is a spiral. You pass through the same territory repeatedly, each time at a deeper level, each time ripping off another layer of the tunic.

The dark cage. The living death. The sentient corpse.

These are not metaphors. They are descriptions. And if you recognize them—if reading these words sends a chill through you because you know exactly what they mean—then you are the sentient corpse becoming aware of its own condition. And that awareness, painful as it is, is the first breath of real life.

12

The Portable Tomb

"The portable tomb, the resident thief."

— CORPUS HERMETICUM VII

The portable tomb. That phrase stopped me in my tracks the first time I read it.

A tomb is a place for the dead. But a portable tomb is a tomb you carry with you. It goes where you go. You do not visit it—you wear it. You are buried alive inside your own life, and you carry the burial with you to every job, every relationship, every city, and every meeting. You cannot run from it because it is strapped to your back. You cannot escape it because it is you.

I was unstable. I had no anchor. I was still running in fight-or-flight mode—an anxious disaster blaming everything outside of me for the sickness I suffered inside. I went from rented room to rented room. From marriage to marriage. From job to job. Nothing I reached for could satisfy the empty space where the truth was supposed to exist. I was looking for home in addresses, in people, in paychecks, and every new place I landed felt exactly like the last one. Because I was not fleeing a place. I was fleeing a tomb. And the tomb was portable.

I define all my trials now as spiritual growing pains. I have no regrets anymore about the past pains that used to haunt me. Each pain I carried into the next relationship, the next city, the next attempt at a life—and each relationship grew more toxic because the unhealed wound was festering, not fading. But I see the purpose now. If the pain had not been great enough, I would have never surrendered. If I had never surrendered, I would have never discovered my remembering. And without the remembering, I would not have the love and the joy I experience today. Some of us, I believe, do not get the spiritual awakening until moments before physical death—and then the shift happens. But by grace, mine came while I still had breath to use it.

When I was thinking about the cover of this book, I decided not to put my name on the front. I do not crave the spotlight. I do not need the world to know who wrote these words. I want the vibration of this message to carry its own weight—to land in your chest not because of who said it, but because of what it is. A name on the cover would make this about me. It is not about me. It is about the truth that moved through me, and truth does not need a signature. For me to be strong enough to write this, I needed to save my soul rather than my face. I needed to take off the mask so you could see the real me, because you cannot love what is hidden. You can only love what is revealed. And if I hid behind a polished version of myself, these words would be just another performance, just another layer.

The world can be critical. I know that. The world will judge this book and the man who wrote it. But that criticism does not define you. It strengthens you eventually. Every stone thrown at the truth only proves the truth was worth throwing stones at. And if my honesty reaches even one person who is drowning in the flood and does not know there is a shore—then every judgment, every raised eyebrow, and every whisper behind my back was worth it. I would rather be naked and real than dressed and dead.

I think about the tumor in physical terms because my body carried it for years. The tension in my jaw. The knot between my shoulder blades. The shallow breathing that I did not know was shallow until someone taught me to breathe from the belly. The body is the tomb's architecture. It records every unprocessed experience, every suppressed emotion, every moment of fight or flight that was never resolved. The body keeps the score, as one author put it, and the score, by the time most people reach the breaking point, is devastating.

I began to address the portable tomb not only through the inner work but also through the body itself. Through movement. Through breathing practices. Through the simple, radical act of feeling what I was feeling instead of numbing it. I discovered that the tomb was not just in my mind. It was in my muscles. In my posture. In the way I held my breath when someone raised their voice. In the way my shoulders climbed toward my ears when I felt unsafe. In the way my entire body constricted around the un-processed material of decades.

The body work was not separate from the spiritual work. It was the same work, addressed from a different angle. Every tension released was a brick removed from the tomb. Every breath taken fully and consciously was a window opened in the portable prison. Every moment of embodied presence—of actually being in my body instead of fleeing from it into thought—was a moment of freedom.

I tell the men I guide to pay attention to their bodies. Not because the body is the answer, but because the body is carrying the question. The unprocessed grief, the unfelt feelings, and the unresolved conflicts—all of it lives in the tissue, in the nervous system, and in the patterns of tension and holding that have become so habitual they feel like the body itself. But they are not the body. They are the tomb. And the tomb can be taken apart, brick by brick, breath by breath, one act of embodied awareness at a time.

The resident thief. This is the companion to the tomb—the thing that lives inside you and steals from you while you sleep. Not a thief who breaks in from outside. A thief who already lives there. A thief was there before you moved in. A thief so embedded in the structure of your inner life that you cannot distinguish his activities from your own.

What does the thief steal? Everything. Joy. Presence. Connection. The ability to be in a moment without reaching for the next one. The ability to love without the fear of loss. The ability to rest without the compulsion to perform. The thief takes these things so quietly that you do not notice until one day you reach for them and they are gone. And you cannot remember when they disappeared because the theft happened so slowly it felt like natural erosion.

Jung described the unconscious as a repository—a vast underground chamber where everything we have not dealt with is stored. The traumas we did not process. The griefs we did not mourn. The truths we did not face. And this repository is not passive. It is active. It reaches up into the conscious mind and pulls things down. It sabotages our plans. It ruins our relationships. It takes what we value most and buries it in the dark.

The wreckage of the past. That is what it is. The accumulated damage of a life lived in the tomb. Every relationship I destroyed. Every opportunity I squandered. Every person I hurt while trying to escape my own pain. The wreckage is not behind me. It is inside me. I carry it.

I have come to believe that the cloak---the tunic---is made of time. Made of the past we refuse to release and the future we refuse to stop grasping. Regret is one thread. Resentment is another. Fear of what might come. Grief for what has gone. The entire covering is woven from our relationship with time, and it covers us so completely that we cannot experience the only moment that is real— this one. Now.

Here.

The tomb is portable because the past is portable. You carry it in your body. In the tension of your shoulders. In the patterns of your breathing. In the way you flinch at certain words or freeze in certain situations. The body remembers everything the mind has tried to forget, and the body becomes the tomb where those memories are buried.

And the thief is resident because the thief is it. Not a demon. Not an external force. The part of you that you have been calling yourself—it, the planner, the worrier, the judge—that is the thief. It lives in your house. It eats your food. It sleeps in your bed. And it takes everything of value and locks it in a room you have never entered.

But here is what I have come to understand about the thief, and it changes everything. The false self is the person who loves the fear of getting caught. It is the game the bank robber plays. He robs one bank successfully, and the adrenaline rush is extraordinary. So, he sets out to do it again. And again. The thrill is not in the money. The thrill is in the game itself—the deception, the control, the feeling of getting away with something. And when the inner deceiver finally gets caught, it pleads innocent. Not guilty. It will deny the robbery while the stolen money is still in its pockets.

But you do not kill it. You do not shame it. You do not exile it. You do not pretend it is evil. You befriend it. You sit it down like a business partner who has been running a shady operation, and you say, look, you are a thief. You have been caught. Just admit it. We can work together now. And the moment it stops denying and hiding, it becomes useful. It becomes honest. It becomes aligned. It becomes a business partner in God's enterprise instead of a con artist running its own.

Think of a wild dog. A wild dog only bites because no one ever taught it how to live in a home. It growls because it is scared. It snaps because it does not understand safety yet. When you finally become the right owner—calm, steady, patient—the dog stops attacking. It starts listening. It starts trusting. It is the same way. It is not evil. It is not the enemy. It has just been running the house without guidance. You do not punish it. You do not beat it. You do not throw it outside. You train it. You teach it. You show it a better way.

And when the narrator finally feels a real master—a loving one— it relaxes. It stops barking at every shadow. It stops biting the hand that feeds it. It becomes loyal, aligned, and useful. A trained dog becomes a companion. A trained mind becomes a servant of God.

The portable tomb. The resident thief.

You are carrying both right now. But the fact that you can see them means you are not them. The seer is not the seen. The one who recognizes the tomb is not the one buried in it.

That distinction is where freedom begins.

Consider the layers, because understanding the layers is the difference between surface recovery and deep awakening.

The first layer is the symptom. The compulsion, the behavior, the coping mechanism that brought you to your knees. Removing this layer is the beginning, and it is essential. Without stopping, nothing else is possible. But removing the symptom is like peeling the outermost skin of an onion. The onion remains.

The second layer is the behavior. The patterns of control, manip-
ulation, dishonesty, and self-destruction that drove the behavior
in the first place. These patterns persist long after the symptom is
removed. I know people with twenty years of recovery who are
still running the same behavioral programs they always ran--- controlling, managing, performing, and hiding. The symptom is
gone, but the machinery is intact.

The third layer is the belief system. The deep, often unconscious
beliefs about who you are and how the world works. I am unlova-
ble. I am defective. I must earn my worth. The world is unsafe.
Trust is dangerous. Vulnerability is weakness. These beliefs were
not chosen. They were installed, usually in childhood, usually by
people who had the same beliefs installed in them. They form the
core of it, the threads that hold everything else together. You can
remove the symptom and change the behavior and still be walking
around in a suit woven from false beliefs.

The fourth layer is identity itself. The belief that you are the sum
of your experiences, your personality, and your story. The belief
that the character you have been playing for your entire life is who
you are. This is the deepest layer of the disguise, and it is the one
that most people never reach. Because to remove this layer is to
remove yourself. Not the true self—the true self cannot be removed.
But the character. The narrated self. The self that is a story rather
than a presence.

When the Hermetic text describes it, it is describing all four layers.
The dark cage is the cage of belief. The living death is the death of

identity mistaken for life. The sentient corpse is the soul that knows it is trapped but does not know which layer is trapping it.

I have worked through these layers in recovery, and the work is not linear. You do not neatly remove one layer, then the next, then the next. You spiral. You encounter the same issues at deeper levels. The resentment you thought you had resolved surfaces again, but this time it is rooted in a belief you had not yet uncovered. The fear you thought you had faced returns, but this time it is attached to an identity you had not yet questioned.

This is why the path is a spiral, not a line. You pass through the same territory repeatedly, but each time you are deeper, each time the layer you are addressing is more fundamental, each time the ripping is more intimate, and the liberation more profound.

The prisons are inside prisons. But so is the freedom. Inside every prison is a smaller prison, and inside every smaller prison is the key that opens the one outside it. The work is to keep going in. Deeper. Past the layers. Past the comfortable stopping points. Past the places where the inner voice says, this is far enough; you have done enough work; you can rest now.

You can rest. But you cannot stop. Because the tomb has layers, and each layer removed reveals the next, and the light at the center—the good that lies within—is only visible when all the layers have been addressed.

Presence deserves its own reflection because it is the antidote to the tomb. The tomb is made of time—past and future, regret, and fear. The only place the tomb does not exist is the present moment. Right now. This breath. This word on this page. The tomb cannot follow you into the now because the tomb is built entirely of then and when.

Every spiritual tradition points to this. Be here now. This is the day the Lord has made. Sufficient unto the day is the evil thereof. The present moment is the only exit from the portable tomb. Not the future—the future is where the fear lives. Not the past—the past is where the regret lives. The present. The only real thing.

I practice presence the way an athlete practices a sport—repetitively, deliberately, failing constantly and trying again. It pulls me into the past. I notice. I come back. It flings me into the future. I notice. I come back. The muscles of presence are weak from years of disuse, and they strengthen slowly, the way any neglected muscle strengthens—through patient, persistent effort.

But each moment of presence is a moment outside the tomb. Each breath taken in full awareness is a breath of free air. Each second spent in the now is a second spent alive—not in the living death, not in the sentient corpse, but genuinely, irreducibly alive.

The tomb is portable. But the present moment is more portable still. You carry it everywhere. It goes where you go. And unlike the tomb, it is made of light.

There is a practice in the recovery community that addresses the resident thief directly, though it is not always understood in these terms. It is the tenth step— the continued personal inventory. Every day, you take stock. Every day, you check the rooms of your house for evidence of theft. Has resentment stolen your peace today? Has fear stolen your courage? Has self-pity stolen your gratitude? Has the thief been at work while you were distracted?

I do this every evening. I sit with the day, and I review it. Not with judgment—that is just the thief wearing a different mask. With awareness. With the calm, clear-eyed attention of a homeowner who knows a thief lives in his house and has learned to check the locks before bed.

Some evenings the inventory is clean. The thief was quiet. The rooms are intact. The peace is where I left it. The courage is where I put it. These are the days when the practices are working, when it is thin, when the present moment is more real than the tomb.

Other evenings the inventory reveals damage. The thief was busy. He stole my patience in the afternoon meeting. He took my compassion during the difficult conversation. He lifted my peace while I was scrolling through the news. And I notice the damage, and I name it, and I do what the program teaches: I admit it, I ask for the defect to be removed, and I make amends where amends are needed. Then I close the day and release it.

This is the daily battle. Not the dramatic, cinematic struggle of early recovery. The quiet, persistent, unglamorous discipline of living with a thief you cannot evict but can learn to watch. The thief does not leave. The pretender does not die. But the relationship changes. The thief becomes less powerful when he is seen. The theft becomes less damaging when it is caught early. And slowly, over years of daily inventory, the rooms of the house become more your own.

I have come to see the tenth step as the spiritual equivalent of hygiene. You do not brush your teeth once and consider the job done. You do it every day because the buildup returns every day. The tomb rebuilds every night. The thief restocks his tools every morning. And the only defense is the daily practice of attention, of naming, of bringing what is hidden into the light.

The portable tomb. The resident thief. They are permanent residents of the human condition. But the present moment is a more permanent resident still. And the present moment, attended to with faithfulness and care, is the room in the house where the thief cannot enter.

13

The Robber In Thy House

"The one who hates through what he loves and envies through what he hates."

— CORPUS HERMETICUM VII

This is the most disorienting line in the entire Hermetic text, and it took me years to understand it.

Hates through what he loves. How do you hate through love? How does desire become destruction?

I will tell you how because I lived it.

I loved what the numbing gave me. I loved it the way a drowning man loves the plank that keeps him afloat—desperately, singularly, with a grip that left marks. And that love destroyed everything it touched. My relationships. My health. My integrity. My capacity for honest connection. The thing I loved most was the thing that was killing me. And I could not let go because I had convinced myself that letting go would be the death of me.

That is the trick of the inner resistance. It attaches you to the things that destroy you and calls the attachment love. It hands you a poison and calls it medicine. It locks you in a cage and calls it home. And you defend the cage because you love it, because the cage is familiar, because the alternative—the open air, the unstructured freedom, the terrifying expanse of a life without walls—is too much to bear.

Envy is what he hates. This is the mirror image. The false self takes the things you claim to despise and generates a secret longing for them. I hated the people who seemed free—the ones who could drink normally, the ones who had their lives together, and the ones who appeared to move through the world without the weight I carried. I told myself I hated them. But the hate was envy wearing a disguise. I wanted what they had. I wanted to be who they were. And because I could not have it, I turned the wanting into contempt.

This is the ego unleashed—consuming everything in its path. It is unchecked, spinning in its own orbit, loving what kills it and hating what could save it. It is the most perfectly inverted psychology imaginable—a system designed to keep you locked in the tomb by making the tomb feel like the only safe place to be.

Jung described the shadow as the part of us that holds everything we reject. But the shadow does not go away when we reject it. It goes underground. It infiltrates our desires. It hijacks our emotions. The shadow is the intruder in the house—the part of us that operates in the dark, stealing from us while we sleep, rearranging our motives so that love becomes destruction and hate becomes longing.

I see this pattern everywhere now. In myself, first. In the same way, I still sometimes reach for the thing that will hurt me and recoil from the thing that will heal me. But also, in the world. In the way entire cultures love what is destroying them—the convenience, the consumption, the endless distraction—and hate what could save them—the silence, the stillness, the confrontation with what is real.

The thief in the house is not a stranger. He is you. The part of you that you have not met yet. The part that operates from the shadows, pulling strings you cannot see, directing your desires toward your own destruction with the quiet efficiency of an embezzler who knows where all the money is kept.

The only way to disarm him is to turn on the lights. To face the shadow. To do the inventory. To say aloud, to another human being, "Here is what lives inside me." Here is the thing that hates through what it loves. Here is the thing that envies through what it hates.

When you name the thief, he begins to lose his power. Not all at once. But enough.

There is a moment in the awakening when you ask to be freed from the patterns that have been running your life. I used to think that meant my sins—the undesirable things I did. But I have come to understand it differently. These patterns are the tools the thief uses to operate. Selfishness is what he uses to steal connection. Fear is what he uses to steal courage. Dishonesty is how he takes intimacy. Resentment is how he robs you of peace. Each one is a key on the thief's ring, and together they open every door in your house.

To ask God to remove them is to ask for the disarming of the thief. Not his destruction— it does not die, not fully, not in this life. But the disarming. The confiscation of the keys. So that the thief still lives in the house, but he can no longer open the doors. He is still present, but he is powerless. He sits in the corner, muttering, while you walk freely through rooms you have never entered.

This is not a one-time prayer. It is a daily request. Because the thief is resourceful. He finds new tools. He develops new mechanisms. He adapts. And the only way to stay ahead of him is to keep asking, keep naming, and keep shining the light into the corners where he hides.

I love the robber now, in a way. Not because I approve of his activities, but because I understand him. He is not evil. He is afraid. It is afraid—afraid of dissolution, afraid of the light, afraid of the vast open space beyond it. And his theft is a form of self-preservation—a desperate attempt to keep control in a universe that was never his to control.

Understanding him does not excuse him. But it allows you to face him without rage, without hatred, without the kind of violent resistance that only makes him stronger. You face him with compassion. You face him with truth. You face him with the quiet confidence of someone who knows that the house belongs to its true owner, and the true owner is not the thief.

My false self-kept me in bondage for years. I used to define my inner self by the way I perceived everyone else was living. This was before I could notice how easily I was being persuaded by appearances—the curated life that humanity wants the world to see. But that is only a skin-deep perspective. To truly know someone's essence, you would have to walk in their shoes first, and I never did that. Instead, I copied them. I exhausted myself focusing on my outward appearance out of sheer terror that you might see my true self. All I wanted was to be loved and accepted, so I learned to be a chameleon. I changed colors for every room I entered. I became whoever I thought you needed me to be, and in the process, I lost any memory of who I was.

When you live by the impostor long enough, the false life is all there seems to be. This is spiritual bankruptcy. You have spent every cent of your inner currency on supporting it, and there is nothing left. You are broken in the only way that truly matters—broke in the soul. But the blessing of spiritual bankruptcy is that it forces you to take inventory. You begin to peel back the layers of the onion, and underneath the performance and the pretending, you discover the liabilities you have been dragging through life. The resentments. The fears. The dishonesty. The desperate need to control how others see you. And one by one, you discard them.

Eventually you are left with your true assets. The light within. And that light does not belong only to those in recovery. It belongs to all of us. From there, you finally have bedrock. You can build a true foundation and grow roots deep enough to weather the storms—like a Florida palm tree during a hurricane, bending but never breaking because the roots go down into something real. And from that foundation, something extraordinary happens. You can match your inside life with your outside life. You stop performing and start living. The chameleon puts down its colors and discovers it was always its own most beautiful shade.

There is something precise about the way hatred works in active suffering because the Hermetic description is exact.

When I was drinking, I loved the people who enabled me and hated the people who confronted me. The people who let me stay asleep were my friends. The people who tried to wake me up were my enemies. My entire relational world was organized around it. Those who helped me keep it on were loved. Those who tried to pull it off were despised. And I did not see the inversion. I could not see it. It had rearranged my perception so thoroughly that the people who were saving me looked like attackers, and the people who were killing me looked like allies.

And the people who poured the drinks, laughed at the jokes that were not funny, pretended that the destruction was entertainment— those people, I kept close. I called them loyal. I called them real. I called them the only ones who understood me.

He does not work alone. He recruits. He builds a network of accomplices who reinforce the theft and who help support the conditions under which the stealing can continue. In recovery, we call them enablers. In psychological terms, they are the co-conspirators of the deceiver within. In Hermetic terms, they are fellow sleepers, dreaming the same dream, stumbling in the same direction, and confirming each other's intoxication.

Breaking free of him means breaking free of his network. It means allowing the relationships that served the false life to fall away and building new relationships that serve the truth. This is one of the most painful aspects of early recovery. You lose friends. You lose the people who were comfortable with you the way you were. You lose the mirror that reflected the image you wanted to see.

But you gain something immeasurably more valuable. You gain people who tell you the truth. People who love you enough to say the thing you do not want to hear. People who will not take part in the theft, who will not enable the stealing, who will you look in the eye and say, I see what is happening, and I will not pretend that I do not.

Those people are the guide's allies. They are the hands extended in the dark. They are the fellowship the Hermetic text describes—the awake ones who gaze with the heart toward the light.

14

That Throttles Thee

"Such is the odious tunic you have put on. It strangles you and drags you down with it so that you will not hate its viciousness."

— CORPUS HERMETICUM VII

You put it on.

That is the detail I keep coming back to. The text does not say the tunic was placed on you. It does not say someone else dressed you in it. It says you put it on. You chose the mask. You wear it voluntarily. And now it is strangling you.

The false self is not a foreign invasion. It is a self-installation. We build our own cages. We weave our own garments. We construct the very walls that imprison us, and we do it so naturally that the construction feels like self-expression.

My personality. My identity. My way of doing things. All of it—the control, the defensiveness, the image management, the relentless need to be right—I put it on. Nobody forced it on me.

And now it strangles me.

The word "strangle" is precise. It does not crush. It does not strike. It squeezes slowly. It tightens in increments so small you do not notice them until the breath is gone. That is exactly how it operates. It does not destroy your life in a single blow. It constricts it gradually, year by year, until the life you are living is so small, so controlled, so devoid of air that you can barely breathe—and you have no idea how you got here.

Every ancient culture understood this. The myths of mermaids and sirens—the Greek sirens, the Celtic Merrows, and the Slavic Rusalki—all describe the same thing. A beautiful voice calling from the water. An enchanting song that lures the sailor off course. The beauty is real. The seduction is real. But beneath the surface waits the drowning. These beings drag their victims to the dark depths, and the victims go willingly, hypnotized by the song. The ancients were not writing fairy tales. They were writing warnings. It is the siren. It is a beautiful song. And the flood is the dark water waiting beneath.

The stark truth of this strangling is that it is like resting in warm water while the temperature rises so slowly you never notice. You sit in the bath, and it feels pleasant. Comfortable. Safe. And degree by degree, the heat increases, and you adjust, and you adjust again, and by the time the water is scalding, you have already lost the ability to feel the burn. It works like ivy on a building. It starts small—a single vine, barely visible, clinging to the brick. And it looks beautiful at first. Charming, even. But the ivy does not stop. It climbs and it spreads and it works its roots into the mortar, and by the time you notice the damage, the ivy is holding the wall together even as it pulls it apart. You cannot remove it without tearing down the structure. That is the disguise. Beautiful on the surface, destructive underneath, and so entangled with the thing it is destroying that removal feels like death.

Drags you down. The tunic is heavy. It pulls you earthward. It keeps you focused on the ground, on the material, on the immediate, and on the tangible. It prevents you from looking up— from lifting your gaze to the thing above you that the text keeps pointing toward. Its gravity is relentless. Every time you try to rise, it pulls. Every time you glimpse the light, it drags you back to the shadow.

But the most devastating part of the text is what follows. So that you will not hate its viciousness. It does not just strangle you—it makes you love the strangling. It convinces you that the constriction is comfort. That the smallness is safety. That the choking is normal.

This is Stockholm syndrome.

I defended my captor for years. I defended my anger because it felt like strength. I defended my isolation because it felt like independence. I defended my numbing because it felt like freedom. Every prison I lived in, I called a castle. Every chain I wore, I called a bracelet. And anyone who tried to show me what was really happening—anyone who pointed at the bars and said, "This is a cage---I pushed them away. Because hating it would mean taking it off. And taking it off would mean standing naked. And standing naked, without the costume, without the identity, without the performance—that was the thing I feared more than death.

I was having a rough time at work some years ago. I was letting the personalities of others destroy my serenity. Every interaction felt like an assault. All office politics felt personal. I was carrying the weight of other people's chaos as if it were my own, and by the time I got in my truck to drive home I was miserable—a healthy man drowning in self-pity. And as I was driving home that day, I noticed a person in a wheelchair on the sidewalk. They were laughing. Not politely. Not performing. Laughing with their whole body, their whole face, their whole being. And something broke open in me. Here I was, healthy, able-bodied, breathing without a machine, walking without aid—and I was miserable. And here was this person, facing a struggle I could not begin to understand, and they were filled with joy. They were living in the moment despite their circumstance. I was dying in the moment because of mine.

I was positioned there to see that message. I know that now. That was not an accident. That was grace arriving in the form of a stranger on a sidewalk, and I was finally awake enough to receive it.

Jung called this identification with the complex. When a psychological pattern becomes so embedded that you cannot distinguish it from yourself, you will defend it as if your life depends on it—because in a sense, your life does depend on it. The false life. The performed life. The life of the tunic. If the tunic comes off, that life ends. And it experiences the removal of the tunic as annihilation.

They call it denial. But "denial" is too mild a word for what happens. Denial implies a passive refusal to see. What it does is active. It reorganizes your perception so that the viciousness looks like virtue. It rewrites the narrative in real time so that the strangling feels like an embrace.

The tunic is odious. The text uses that word deliberately. It is vile. It is repulsive. But you must see it clearly before you can hate it. And seeing it clearly requires the very eyes the tunic was designed to blind.

This is the paradox at the heart of the awakening. You need to see the cage to leave it. But the cage is designed to prevent you from seeing it.

The only exit is grace. The only break in the loop is something from outside the loop reaching in.

I have thought about grace more than almost anything else in my recovery. What is it? Where does it come from? Why does it arrive for some people and seem to pass others by? I do not have answers. But I have observations. Grace comes in the gratitude. It arrives when you stop demanding that the world be different and start being thankful for what it already is. Grace comes not from the human-doing but from the human-being. Not from the striving, the performing, and the relentless effort to earn your place—but from the simple act of being present, being still, being alive to the moment exactly as it is. You do not wait for the fruitage of the garden. You become the fruitage of the garden in the daily practice. You stop asking when the harvest will come, and you realize that you are the harvest. Every breath of gratitude, every moment of presence, every act of surrender—that is the fruit. It has been growing all along.

Grace comes uninvited. Every spiritual experience I have had—every moment of clean light, every crack, every instant when it loosened and I caught a glimpse of what lay beneath— came when I was not looking for it. Not when I was trying hardest. Not when I was performing my best. Often when I was at my worst— exhausted, broken, on the floor, out of options. Grace does not reward effort. Grace responds to surrender. Grace fills the space that opens when the pretender finally, reluctantly, and exhaustedly lets go.

Grace is always present. It is always flowing, always available, always pressing against the walls, looking for cracks. The problem is not the supply of grace. The problem is the resistance to it. It is it. It is the resistance. The plot, the cage, the tomb, the thief—all of it is resistance to the grace that is trying to reach you.

This is why the ripping matters. Not because you earn the light by removing what covers you. But because what covers you is what blocks the light. The light is already shining. It has always been shining. You do not need to create it. You only need to stop obstructing it.

Grace is not a reward. It is raining. It falls on everyone equally. But the soul with an open heart gets wet, and the soul sealed in the covering stays dry. The rain does not discriminate. The tunic does.

I have watched grace arrive in the most unlikely places. In a prison meeting where a man with a face like a clenched fist suddenly broke open and wept. In a hospital room where a woman who had lost everything put her head on the table and said, "I cannot do this anymore," and in the saying of it, found that she could. In the parking lot after a meeting where someone who had been silent for months suddenly turned to me and said something so true, so precise, and so clearly delivered from somewhere beyond their ordinary thinking that we both stood still, stunned by the weight of it.

Grace does not arrive on schedule. It does not follow a formula. It does not reward the deserving and bypass the unworthy. It arrives when the conditions are right—when the grip has been loosened enough, when the hands have opened enough, when it has exhausted itself enough to stop blocking the rain.

What I understand now is that the entire program of recovery is a technology for making the conditions right. The work does not earn grace. It removes the obstacles to it. The inventory loosens it. The confession opens the hands. The amends clear the channel. The prayer and meditation create the silence in which the still small voice can be heard. None of it produces the grace. All of it makes room for it.

This is why I say the program is a mystical technology. Not because it is mystical in the way people usually mean—all incense and crystals and vague feelings of cosmic oneness. Because it is a systematic method for removing the barriers between the human soul and the grace that is always flowing. It is engineering applied to the spirit. It is a repeatable, testable, demonstrable process by which a person moves from sealed to open, from dry to drenched, and from asleep to awake.

And it works. Not perfectly. Not for everyone. Not on any predictable timeline. But it works. I have watched it work in hundreds of people. I have felt it work in myself. The wrapping loosens. The rain comes in. The soul, parched from decades of self-imposed drought, drinks deeply for the first time. And the drinking—the real drinking, the drinking of grace instead of poison—is the thing the thirst was always for.

The strangulation loosens. The plot unravels. It is that convinced you it was your skin that begins to feel like what it is—a covering, an addition, a thing that was put on and can be taken off.

And beneath it, the rain-soaked soul, finally feeling what it was always meant to feel.

15

The Beauty of the Truth

"Not look up and see the fair vision of truth and the good that lies within."

— CORPUS HERMETICUM VII

The cloak prevents one thing more than anything else. It prevents you from looking up.

Not out. Not around. Up. The direction matters. Down is where it lives—in the material, the earthbound, and the heavy. Up is where the truth waits—not in some literal sky, but in the higher registers of consciousness that it is specifically designed to block.

The fair vision of truth. The text calls truth fair. Beautiful. Desirable. This is not the grim truth of the courtroom or the doctor's office. This is not truth as punishment. This is truth as beauty—the most beautiful thing there is. The truth is not something to be endured. It is something to be seen, the way you see a sunrise. It takes your breath away.

I did not believe that for a long time. I thought truth was harsh. I thought truth was the thing that hurt. I thought truth was the moral inventory, the fearless look at the wreckage, and the confession of everything I had done. And it is that. But it is also more than that. The truth beneath the wreckage, the truth at the bottom of the inventory, the truth you find after you have ripped it off and stood naked in the light—that truth is beautiful.

The good that lies within. Within what? Within you. The good is not somewhere else. It is not in a distant heaven or a future life or a different body. It is inside the very person who has been wearing the cloak. Underneath the ignorance, underneath the vice, underneath the decades of forgetting—there is a good so fundamental that it cannot be destroyed. It can only be covered.

Jung called this integration. The moment when the shadow has been faced, the persona has been removed, and the Self—the whole, authentic center—emerges. He said it was not the creation of something new. It was the discovery of something that had always been there.

Integration is not assembly. It is unveiling.

The spiritual awakening is this seeing. It is the moment when the veil is thin enough that you glimpse what lives behind it. And what lives behind it is not the darkness you feared. It is light. It is the good that lies within. It is the image of the Divine that you were made in, still intact, still shining, despite everything you have piled on top of it.

Siddhartha Gautama—the man who would become the Buddha—sat beneath a Bodhi tree and vowed not to rise until he had seen the truth. The stories say he was tempted. The stories say he was attacked by every fear and desire the mind could produce. But he did not move. He sat with all of it. He let the storm rage, and he did not flinch. And when the storm passed, what remained was not a new thought or a new belief. It was a seeing. A clarity that did not come from thinking. A peace that did not come from circumstances. He saw, with perfect stillness, the nature of things as they are. And the seeing changed everything.

My Bodhi tree was a concrete floor.

I was lying on that cold concrete jail floor, and something in me shattered open. It felt like the stars collided inside my chest—not out in the sky, but in me. There was no comfort, no cushion, no incense. Just fluorescent lights and steel bars and the rawness of existence stripped of every pretense. It had been ripped off by circumstances I could no longer control. I had nothing left. No image to protect. No performance to support. No audience to impress. Just a man on a floor, finally empty enough for the truth to enter.

And in that rawness, something ancient woke up. A clarity that did not come from thinking. A peace that did not come from circumstances. It was like remembering something I had always known but had forgotten—the way you remember your own name after a fever breaks. The universe whispered what it had been whispering all along, only now I was quiet enough to hear it: you were never alone. You were never broken. You were always the light. That concrete floor became my Bodhi tree. That moment became my awakening.

And I wept. Because I had spent my entire life believing I was defective. Believing it was the real me. Believing the cage was my home.

And in that one moment of sight, the lie collapsed. Not the pain—the pain was still there. Not the past—the past was still real. But the lie that the pain and the past defined me—that lie died in the seeing.

I had been so afraid. Afraid of the truth, afraid of the emptiness, afraid of what I would find if I stopped running. But when you finally face your fear—when you walk straight into it instead of around it— --You pass right through it and discover it was only a mirage. An oasis shimmering on the desert horizon that disappears the moment you arrive. The fear was never real. It was its last defense. And once you walk past it, you realize the only thing on the other side of fear is freedom.

Once you see it, the old life becomes impossible. That is what I want to tell you. Once you have glimpsed the fair vision of truth, you cannot go back. You can forget again—and you will, for periods—but you cannot un-see. The image is burned into you. The beauty of the truth has marked you. And from that moment forward, every time the false skin tightens, you will remember that it is not you.

Look up. The good is there. The good is within. It has been waiting for you longer than you know.

I think about what happens in the world when one person sees the truth. It is not anything. It is not a private event that affects only the seer. When one person sees the good that lies within, the seeing itself becomes a kind of transmission. It radiates outward. Not through words, not through teaching, not through any deliberate act of communication—but through the quality of presence that goes with the seeing.

You have met people like this. People who walk into a room and the room changes. Not because they say anything brilliant. Not because they perform. Because they carry something. A weight that is not heavy but dense. A gravity that draws you in. A steadiness that makes the anxious mind fall quiet. These are people who have seen the fair vision of truth, and the seeing has changed them, and the change in them changes the atmosphere around them.

This is what it means to carry the message. The message is not words. The message is the change. The message is the quality of being that emerges when it has been removed and the good within has been seen. You carry the message by being the message. You transmit the truth by being transformed by the truth.

I am not there yet. Not fully. Not consistently. But I have moments. And in those moments, I notice something remarkable: other people respond. Not to what I say, but to what I am. They lean in. They listen differently. They put down their defenses. Something in them recognizes something in me—not because I am special, but because what I carry is what they carry too, buried under their own version of it, waiting to be seen.

The fair vision of truth is not private. It is contagious. One person seeing it makes it easier for the next person to see it. The light multiplies. The seeing spreads. And slowly, slowly, the illusion thins.

I think about the moment I described—the early morning, the silence, the collapse of the noise—and I want to add something I did not say then. What I saw in that moment was not only good. It was also small. The good that lies within is not grand in the way it imagines grandeur. It is not spectacular. It is not impressive. It is simple. It is the basic, irreducible goodness of a soul that was made by something good and has never stopped being what it was made to be.

This is why it misses it. It is looking for fireworks. It wants the spiritual experience to be dramatic, extraordinary, and something worth posting about. But the good that lies within is quiet. It is the goodness of a heartbeat. The goodness of a breath taken without thinking. The goodness of the cells that repair themselves while you sleep. It is so ordinary, so fundamental, so woven into the fabric of your existence that you have been looking past it your entire life, searching the horizon for something that was in your chest all along.

The mystics describe this as the ground of being. Not the peak of being—the ground. The foundation. The thing that was there before anything was built on top of it and will be there after everything built on top of it has fallen away. You cannot achieve the ground. You can only sink to it. And you can only sink to it by releasing everything you are holding onto—every accomplishment, every identity, and every image of yourself that is not the ground itself.

I think about the people in the rooms that have the most light. They are not, in my experience, the most articulate or the most educated or the most successful. They are the ones who have sunk the deepest. The ones who lost the most. The ones who had everything stripped away until all that remained was the ground. And from the ground, they radiate a warmth that has nothing to do with personality and everything to do with presence.

You cannot manufacture this warmth. You cannot study your way to it. You cannot perform it. It is the natural emission of a soul that has been uncovered. It is what the sun does—shines— not because it is trying to, but because shining is what it is.

The fair vision of truth is the discovery that you are, at your foundation, made of light. Not the dramatic, blinding light of religious ecstasy. The quiet, steady, unremarkable light of a soul that was good before it was covered and is good still.

Look up. Look in. The light is there.

16

The Plot Against Thee

"Not understanding the plot that it has plotted against you when it made insensible the organs of sense."

— CORPUS HERMETICUM VII

There is a plot against you.

That sounds paranoid. I know how it sounds. But the text does not whisper this. It says it plainly. The covering of ignorance has plotted against you. It is not a passive covering. It is an active conspiracy. It has a strategy. It has a method. And its method is precise: it makes insensible the organs of sense.

The plot is to numb you. Not to harm you—that would be too obvious. Not to kill you—that would end the game. But to numb you.

To make the instruments by which you perceive reality insensible, inapparent, and unrecognized for what they are. To leave you alive but unable to feel. Awake but unable to see. Equipped with every organ of sense and unable to use one.

I think about this in terms of my own life. I was born with the capacity to perceive the sacred. Every human being is. We come into the world with eyes that can see beauty, hearts that can feel truth, and minds that can apprehend the infinite. And then the world goes to work. Layer by layer, the organs are dulled. Fear and shame are installed. The relentless message that you are nothing more than a body, nothing more than an economic unit, nothing more than a consumer—this message is installed so deeply that by the time you are an adult, the organs of perception that were meant to see God are as atrophied as muscles that have never been used.

It does this. Not maliciously, perhaps. It is a survival mechanism. Its job is to navigate the material world, to protect the body, and to manage threats. But a survival mechanism that has taken over the entire operation is no longer a tool—it is a tyrant. And this tyrant's first act is to end any feeling that threatens its reign. The perception of the soul threatens it. The perception of the Divine threatens it. The belief that you are more than a body in a world of bodies threatens it. And so, it numbs those beliefs. Not with violence. With noise. With busyness. With the relentless consumption that keeps the organs stuffed and the mind distracted.

Jung called these the defenses of the false self. Denial. Projection. Rationalization. Intellectualization. Every one of them serves the same purpose—to keep you from seeing what is real. They are not signs of intelligence. They are signs of the plot. The inner deceiver is defending its position by making you unable to perceive the truth that would dethrone it.

"Denial" is a word used so often in recovery that it has lost some of its power. But denial is not simply refusing to admit you have a problem. Denial is a comprehensive, systematic blindness—a restructuring of perception so thorough that the denied reality does not even appear as a possibility. You do not see it and refuse to believe it. You do not see it. The organs that would detect it have been made insensible.

The conspiracy was inside me all along. That is the revelation. There was no external enemy. No cabal of villains keeping me down. The plot was an inside job—my own false self, my own defenses, and my own fear conspiring to keep me numb enough to survive but not awake enough to live.

And the most terrifying part is that the plot works. It works so well that most people never suspect it. They go through their entire lives with numbed organs, perceiving only what they are allowed to perceive, and they call this perception reality.

But the text reveals the plot. And once you see the conspiracy, you can begin to dismantle it. Not by fighting it—that only strengthens it. But by using the organs, it tried to numb. By looking with the heart. By listening with the inner ear. By waking up the faculties that were put to sleep.

The plot is real. But so is your power to undo it.

I think about children, and it breaks my heart. Children come into the world with the organs of sense wide open. They see everything. They feel everything. They perceive the sacred in a blade of grass, in a shadow on the wall, and in the face of a stranger. And then we educate them.

We socialize them. We teach them to narrow their feeling until it fits inside the cage we have prepared for them.

We do not do this maliciously. We do it because we were caged ourselves, and we do not know any other way. The parents cage the children because the parents were caged by their parents. The teachers cage the students because the teachers were caged by their teachers. The plot is multigenerational. It is ancestral. It is embedded in the very structures of civilization.

But the plot can be undone. Not for everyone at once—the Hermetic text already told us that. But for those who have the power. For those who have been cracked open by pain or grace or both. For those, whose organs of sense, despite the numbing, keep a flicker of their original sensitivity? For those reading this book.

The undoing begins with awareness. You cannot dismantle a conspiracy you do not know exists. But once you see it—once you recognize the plot for what it is, once you notice the numbing as it happens in real time—the plot begins to fail. Awareness is the immune response. Consciousness is the antibody. The simple act of noticing, "Oh, there it is again, the narrator numbing me, it is tightening, the organs shutting down"—that noticing is the beginning of the end.

I practice a form of awareness throughout the day that I was not taught in the rooms but that I have found to be one of the most powerful tools for undoing the plot. I call it catching the numbing.

It works like this: whenever I notice my awareness narrowing—whenever the world begins to flatten, whenever my perception starts to contract into the small box of my habitual thinking—I pause. I notice the contraction. And I ask myself, what am I avoiding?

The answer is always something I do not want to feel. Some discomfort, some vulnerability, some truth that it finds threatening. The numbing is a reflexive response to threat— the automatic dimming of the organs of sense to protect them from exposure. And the simple act of catching it—of noticing, "Oh, there it is, the plot in action"—interrupts the mechanism.

I do not always succeed. The plot is sophisticated. It has been running for decades. It has backup systems and redundancies and layers of defense that can absorb a great deal of awareness before they fail. Some days the numbing wins. Some days I walk through entire hours in the contracted state, perceiving nothing, feeling nothing, a sentient corpse going through the motions.

But increasingly often, I catch it. More often, the awareness fires before the numbing completes. And in that gap—in the space between the attempt to numb and my awareness of the attempt—something opens. A window. A crack. There is a brief, shining moment when the organs of senses reactivate, allowing me to perceive the world, vivid, immediate, and unbearably beautiful.

Those moments are what the Hermetic text is pointing toward. Those moments are the portals of knowledge. They are not distant, mystical experiences reserved for monks on mountaintops.

They are available right now, right here, in the middle of your or-dinary life, whenever you catch the plot and refuse to take part in it.

The plot depends on your unconsciousness. It cannot operate in the light of awareness. It is like a thief who can only steal in the dark. Turn on the light, and the theft stops. Not permanently—the thief will wait for the light to go out and try again. But for this moment, for this breath, for this act of seeing, the plot is undone.

And each undoing strengthens the capacity for the next one. The organs of sense, like any muscle, grow stronger with use. The aware-ness becomes quicker. The catching becomes more reflexive. And slowly, the plot loses ground. Not all at once. But enough.

17

Blocked and Crammed

We are stuffed so full we cannot receive.

That is the condition the text describes, and it is the condition of
the modern world distilled to a single sentence. Blocked up with a
great load of matter. Jammed full of loathsome pleasure. The organs
of perception are not broken. They are obstructed. Packed with so
much material that there is no room for the immaterial. Crammed
with so much pleasure that the deeper satisfaction cannot enter.

I think about my life before recovery. I was not empty. I was the
opposite of empty. I was full.

Full of substances. Full of plans. Full of noise. Full of opinions,
entertainments, obligations, and desires. My inner life was a closet
jammed to the ceiling, and there was no room for one more thing.
And the one thing that needed to enter— the one thing that could
have saved me—could not get in because every available space was
already occupied.

Matter. The material world. The great load. I do not think the text is condemning matter itself. Bodies are not evil. The physical world is not a mistake. But matter becomes an obstruction when it is mistaken for the whole. When the material world fills your entire field of vision, when the only things you pursue are things you can touch, taste, and accumulate, the material becomes a wall. And behind the wall, invisible, starving for your attention, is everything that matters.

Loathsome pleasure. That phrase disturbed me when I first read it. I thought pleasure was good. I had spent my life pursuing it. But the text distinguishes between genuine satisfaction and the counterfeit the world offers. Loathsome pleasure is pleasure that leaves you sick. It is the third drink that crosses the line from relaxation to obliteration. It is the mindless scrolling that fills an hour but empties the soul. It is the consumption of anything—food, sex, entertainment, substances—past the point of enjoyment into the territory of numbing.

I was jammed full of it. I filled every silence with noise. I filled every empty hour with activity. I filled every moment of discomfort with some form of pleasure that promised relief and delivered only more hunger. And the more I consumed, the less I could feel. The organs were blocked. The channels were clogged. The capacity to receive anything real—beauty, truth, grace, the presence of the Divine—was buried under the accumulated weight of everything I had used to avoid it.

Jung understood materialism as a form of spiritual inflation—it expanding to fill the entire psyche, leaving no room for the deeper self. When the inner resistance claims all available territory, the soul has nowhere to breathe. The inner world becomes as cluttered as the outer, and the person lives in a condition of spiritual suffocation—full to bursting and starving to death.

The central problem is this: the things that block us from God. The blockage is not the absence of God. God is there. The light is there. The truth is there. But we have so much on top of it that we cannot see, feel, or hear it. The problem is not the signal. The problem is the noise.

Recovery taught me to empty. To clear the channel. To take things out instead of putting things in. Fasting from substances, yes. But also fasting from noise. Fasting from opinion. Fasting from the relentless need to fill every gap. Silence is not empty. Silence is the only space in which the voice you need to hear can be heard.

We are stuffed so full we cannot receive. The solution is not more. It is less. Not addition, but subtraction. Not getting but releasing.

Make room. The thing you have been looking for has been trying to reach you. But first, you must clear the way.

There is a practice in the monastic traditions called kenosis—self-emptying.

It is the deliberate release of everything that fills the inner space: opinions, attachments, certainties, desires, and fears. Not because these things are evil, but because they take up room.

And the room they take up is the room that the Divine needs in order to enter.

I practice a small version of this every morning. I sit in silence before the day begins, and I let things go. Not by force. By attention. I notice what I am carrying—the worry about the meeting, the resentment about the email, the fear about the money, the plan. I am rehearsing for the tenth time—and I set each one down. Not forever. Just for now. Just for this hour. Just long enough for the space to open and the signal to come through.

Most mornings, nothing dramatic happens. The silence is just silence. The emptiness is just emptiness. But every now and then— maybe once a week, maybe once a month—something enters the space that could not have entered if the space were full. A knowing. Peace. A sense of rightness so profound it brings tears. Not because anything changed. Because I made room for what was already there.

The mystics call this the prayer of quiet. The moment when the striving stops and the receiving begins. The moment when you stop trying to reach God and allow God to reach you. It requires nothing but emptiness. And emptiness, in a world that is terrified of it, is the rarest and most courageous offering.

Something happens when you begin to empty. The world notices. The people around you notice. And they do not always respond well.

When you stop consuming at the rate the world expects—when you turn off the television, put down the phone, decline the invitation, and sit in the silence instead of filling it—people become uncomfortable. Your emptiness confronts their fullness. Your stillness exposes their noise.

Your refusal to take part in the collective stuffing is experienced, by those who are still stuffed, as a judgment. Even when it is not.

I lost friendships over this. People who could not understand why I no longer wanted to spend Saturday night the way we used to. People who took my withdrawal from consumption as a rejection of them. People for whom the shared experience of being stuffed was the foundation of the relationship, and when the stuffing stopped, the relationship had nothing left to stand on.

This is one of the costs of the path. The emptying does not happen in a vacuum. It happens in a world that is organized around fullness. The economy depends on your consumption. The culture depends on your participation. The social fabric depends on your willingness to be jammed full of the same loathsome pleasures that keep everyone else jammed. When you step out of that system, you become visible. And visibility, inside it, is dangerous.

But the emptying is not loss. I need to say that clearly. The friendships that ended were not friendships of depth. They were friendships of shared anesthesia. The activities that fell away were not activities of meaning. They were activities of avoidance. What remained, after the emptying, was less—but what remained was real. The handful of people who stayed. The few activities that nourished rather than numbed. The silence that, once feared, became the most valued companion of my day.

Less is the beginning of everything. The mystics understood this. The desert fathers understood this. The minimalist traditions of Zen and the radical simplicity of the early Franciscans—all of these are expressions of the same truth the Hermetic text describes. You must be emptied to be filled. You must make room for the rain.

I think about the instruction to seek conscious contact with God through prayer and meditation. Conscious contact requires space. It requires an inner room that has been cleared of clutter. It requires the willingness to sit with nothing and discover that nothing is not nothing. Nothing is the space in which everything that matters can appear.

Make room. That is the teaching. Make room in your life, in your mind, in your schedule, and in your soul. Clear the clutter. Empty the vessel. And then sit with the emptiness and wait.

What comes to fill it will not be what you expected. It will be better.

18

So That You Do Not Hear

"So that you do not hear what you must hear nor observe what you must observe."

— CORPUS HERMETICUM VII

There are things you must hear.

The text does not say things you might enjoy hearing. Not things that would be nice to hear. Things you must hear. There is an imperative in it—a necessity that is not optional. There are truths your soul needs the way your lungs require air. And the entire structure of it all—the ignorance, the vice, the cage, the tomb, the thief, the plot—exists for one purpose: to prevent you from hearing them.

What are the things I must hear? I have been turning this question over for years, and the answer is simpler than I expected. I must hear that I am not alone. I must hear that I am not my mistakes. I must hear that there is a love holding this entire reality together and that I have never, for a single moment, been outside of it. I must hear that the door is open. I must hear that the light is on. I must hear that everything I thought I had to earn was given freely from the beginning.

And I could not hear any of it. For years. For decades. The false skin blocked the sound. The noise of my own thinking drowned out the signal. The loathsome pleasure stuffed my ears with cotton. I was a radio designed to receive a specific frequency, and every dial was jammed.

Things you must see. Not wanting to see. Must. There are things that exist—right now, precisely here, in the room where you are sitting, in the sky above your head, in the space behind your sternum—that you were designed to see. You have organs for it. You have equipment for it. You were built for perception. And the disguise has disabled every one of them.

Jung called the default state of human consciousness unconsciousness. That is the most damning assessment possible. We are, by default, asleep. The system is designed so that unless something intervenes—unless some crisis, grace, or catastrophe cracks it—we will sleep through our entire lives.

This is the darkest truth in the entire Hermetic text, and it is the one I resist most. I want to believe that most people are awake. I want to believe that consciousness is the norm and unconsciousness the exception. But my experience tells me otherwise. Most of the people

I have known-intelligent, kind, well-intentioned people—are asleep. They are still asleep. They are following the scripts. They are drowning in the flood and calling it swimming. And they do not know it. They cannot know it, because it has made insensible the very organs that would detect their condition.

Some were broken open by pain so severe it cracked, and the light leaked in. Some were softened slowly by grace until the mask loosened on its own. Some hit the wall so hard that the painted sky fell in pieces around them, and they could see, for the first time, that the sky was paint and the wall was real. But awakening does not belong only to the shattered. It belongs to anyone willing to look up. The door is not locked. It never was. It opens from the inside, and it opens for everyone—sufferer or saint, broken or whole, religious, or not. The only requirement is the willingness to see.

This is the terrible gift of suffering, of trauma, of catastrophe. It breaks it all open. It cracks through. It creates, through destruction, the opening through which grace can enter.

I would not wish my suffering on anyone. But I would not trade it either. Because my suffering broke me. And the breaking let the light in.

Recovery calls it a sickness of the spirit. This condition presents as a persistent state of unease, characterized by restlessness without a cause, agitation without provocation, and dissatisfaction without a remedy. The person with this sickness feels wrong without knowing what is wrong. It feels like something is missing without knowing it. Feels a hunger that nothing in the material world can satisfy. The feeling is the condition of the blocked and crammed—the organs stuffed, the channels closed, the signal jammed.

We were built to hear and see. That is what I have come to believe. We are not broken machines. We are perfectly designed instruments that have been covered, blocked, numbed, and stuffed until we can no longer perform our function. The function is perception. The perception of the real. The hearing of the truth. The seeing of the good that lies within.

It did not destroy the instruments. It disabled them. The difference matters. A destroyed instrument cannot be repaired. A disabled instrument can be reactivated. The ears still work. The eyes of the heart still function. The capacity to hear what you must hear and see what you must see is still inside you, dormant, waiting, like a seed in winter.

This entire book has been about one thing. The removal of what prevents you from hearing and seeing. The ripping off it. The emptying of the space. The clearing of the channel.

Because there are things you must hear. And they are being spoken. Right now. At this very moment.

The only question is whether you will unblock the ears that can hear them.

I want to leave you with this thought, because it is the thought that changed everything for me. The instruments are not broken. They are covered. The eyes of the heart are not blind. They are blocked. The ears of the soul are not deaf. They are stuffed. You are not a defective machine in need of repair. You are a perfect instrument in need of uncovering.

This means that the work of awakening is not the addition of something you do not have. It is the removal of what is in the way. You do not need to become someone new. You need to discard everything you are not. You do not need to acquire spiritual abilities. You need to recover the abilities you were born with and have been systematically taught to forget.

This is the most hopeful message I have ever remembered. It means the good is already within you. The capacity is already there. The door has already been built into the false reality. You do not need to construct anything. You do not need to earn anything. You just need to do what this book says: take off the costume, empty the vessel, unblock the ears, and open the heart's eyes.

And then listen. Really listen. Its ears hear only what they want to hear. With the ears that were designed for truth. With the organs of sense that the covering tried to disable but could not destroy.

They are still there. They have been waiting your entire life. And the signal they were designed to receive has been broadcasting without interruption since before you were born.

All you have to do is tune in.

I want to sit with the word "must" before this chapter ends, as it carries a weight that cannot be ignored.

The text does not say there are things you might enjoy hearing. It does not say there are optional truths available for your consideration. It says must. There are things you must hear. There are things you must observe. The imperative is absolute. The requirement is nonnegotiable.

There are frequencies your soul requires the way your body needs oxygen. You can live without hearing them—in the technical sense of biological survival—but the life you live without them is the living death the text has already described.

I think about the people I have known who stopped the behavior but never woke up. They stopped the behavior, and they never went back to it. But they never tuned in. They never unblocked the organs. They lived their remaining years in the dry version of the cage—cleaner, quieter, more presentable, but still a cage. And the tragedy is not that they failed. The tragedy is that they came so close. They walked all the way to the door and stood in front of it and never turned the handle.

The things you must hear are not secrets. They are not hidden in ancient texts or locked in the vaults of esoteric traditions. They are being spoken in the wind, in your breath, in the eyes of the stranger who holds the door for you, and in the silence between the notes of the song. The truth is broadcasting on every frequency. The signal is everywhere. The only thing preventing reception is it.

This entire book has been about one thing. Not what covers us—though it has been described in detail? The focus has not been on the truth, despite every chapter pointing towards it. This book has been about the space between the two. The gap. The static. The interference. The distance between what you are hearing and what you must hear.

And the message of this book, if it can be reduced to a single sentence, is this: the distance is not as great as you think. It is not as thick as it feels. The organs are not as dead as they seem. You are closer to the truth than you have ever been.

Tune in.

The Keystone

The root of the problem lies in the worship of self. Not the substance. Not the behavior. Not the external circumstances of a broken life. The insistence on being the center. The relentless, exhausting belief that if I can just arrange the world to my liking, everything will be fine.

It never was fine. It never could be fine. Because the architect of the arrangement was the problem. The builder was broken. The planner was insane. And no amount of rearranging the furniture changes the fact that the house is on fire.

The solution is a keystone—the stone at the top of an arch that holds everything else in place. Without it, the arch collapses. With it, the arch stands. And the keystone is this: that we lay down the throne we were never meant to sit on.

Quit playing God.

That is the whole teaching. The Hermetic text, the Jungian framework, the recovery path— trust God, clean house, help others—and the mystics across every tradition---they all arrive at the same place. You are not God. You are not the director of the show. You are not the architect of reality. And the moment you stop pretending to be—the moment you lay down the role that has been strangling you, dragging you down, and blocking your every organ of perception—the arch appears. The door opens. The light comes in.

I think about what it means to lay down the throne. It does not mean passivity. It does not mean giving up. It means alignment. It means saying, "Your purpose is more important than mine."" It means opening your hands instead of clenching your fists. It means trusting that the intelligence that built the universe can manage the details of your life better than you can.

This is the handshake with God that I never knew I needed. Not a negotiation. Not a contract. A handshake. Two wills meeting—one infinite, one finite—and the finite one finally saying, "I trust you." I will follow. I will stop insisting that I know better.

Walking through the door is the easiest and hardest thing I have ever done. Easy because the door was always open. Hard because walking through it meant leaving behind everything I thought I was. Every identity. Every pretension. Every carefully assembled version of myself that I had been presenting to the world for my entire adult life.

Walking through the door means walking naked into the unknown, with nothing but the old skin you just ripped off lying in a heap behind you.

The angels are watching. I believe that. Not as a metaphor. Not as a comforting idea. As a truth. There is rejoicing in the presence of the angels of God over one sinner who repents. Every soul that wakes up—every Truman who finds the stairs, every sufferer who surrenders, every sleepwalker who opens their eyes—sends a ripple through a realm we cannot see. And the beings in that realm celebrate. Not because we earned it. Because we came home.

Because the thing that was lost was found. Because the prodigal, after wandering through every country of the resistance, finally turned his face toward the father's house.

I think about the rejoicing often. I think about it because it reframes the entire story. We tell the story of recovery as a human achievement—the triumph of will, the conquest of suffering, and the hard-won victory of the one recovering. And it is all those things. But the Hermetic text, the Gospel of Luke, and the mystics of every tradition suggest something larger. They suggest that the awakening of a single soul is an event that reverberates beyond the visible world. That what happens inside a church basement or a hospital room or a lonely apartment at three in the morning is witnessed by beings we cannot see. That the universe itself responds to the opening of a human heart.

This is not something I can prove. It is something I have felt. In the deepest moments of prayer, in the most surrendered moments of silence, I have felt—not believed, not theorized, but felt—the presence of something rejoicing. Something that is not me. Something that is delighted, genuinely delighted, that I showed up. That I walked through. That I am here.

The narrow path. This is not a path of deprivation. It is a path of precision. It is narrow because it does not wander. It goes straight to the door. The broad road meanders through every distraction, every detour, and every loathsome pleasure. The narrow road by-passes all of it. Not because pleasure is evil, but because you have somewhere to be. And the somewhere is more beautiful than anything the broad road offers.

I stand now at the bottom of the ladder, helping others up. That is the final instruction. Once you have been awakened, you reach back. Not to hoard the light. Not to sit in the clean air and congratulate ourselves. To go back. To reach down. I aim to guide others, in the same manner as I was guided, towards the gateways of knowledge.

That is why I wrote this book. Not because I have arrived. Not because I have all the answers. Because someone showed me the door, and I cannot keep it to myself. The guide who led me did not make it to the portals alone. Someone led him. And someone led that person. The chain goes back through centuries, through the rooms, through Jung, through the Hermetics, through the mystics, the saints, and the drunks who fell to their knees and were caught by something they could not name.

I am one link in that chain. This book is my hand, extended. If you can feel it, take it.

I wrote this book in the early mornings, before the world woke up, in the silence where the words come from somewhere other than my mind. I did not outline it. I did not plan it. I sat down with the Hermetic text and the collected works of Jung spread around me like a circle of witnesses, and I wrote what came. Some mornings the words flowed like water. Some mornings they came one at a time, dragged from the silence like stones from a well. But they came. They always came. Because the words are not mine. They belong to the same tradition that produced the Hermetic text and the recovery tradition and Jung's insight into the spiritual thirst. They belong to the chain. I am merely the most recent set of hands through which they pass.

If these words have reached you—if they have bypassed your intellect and landed in your chest, in the place where the eyes of the heart live—then the chain is working. The transmission is alive. The guide's hand is extended across millennia of human darkness, and you are close enough to feel it.

Take it. Not tomorrow. Not when you are ready. Not when you have figured it out. Now. In this moment. With whatever willingness you have, however small, however fragile, however riddled with doubt.

The door does not require certainty. It requires a step.

I want to say one final thing about the Hermetic text that has structured this book. It is not a comfortable text. It does not soothe. It does not reassure. It confronts. It grabs you by the collar the way my shepherd grabbed me and says, "Wake up." Not gently. Urgently. With the voice of someone who can see that the house is on fire and the occupants are sleeping.

That urgency is not cruelty. It is love. The fiercest kind of love--- the love that would rather hurt you with the truth than comfort you with a lie. The love that shakes you awake even though you want to keep sleeping, because the alternative to waking is perishing in the flames.

I have tried, in this book, to honor that urgency. I have tried to speak with the same directness, refusal to sugarcoat, and fierce compassion as the Hermetic author did in his ancient sermon. Because the same conditions that prompted his cry still exist. The flood is still flowing. The veil is still covering. The organs are still blocked. The plot is still operative. And the people—you people, as the text so bluntly addresses its audience—are still stumbling in the dark.

But the door is also still open. The light is also still shining. The guide is also still reaching back. And the signal—the thing you must hear, the truth you must observe—is also still broadcasting, patient and persistent, waiting for the moment when the static clears and the reception begins.

If this book has been the clearing of even a little static, then it has done what it was meant to do. If it has loosened a thread, unblocked a sense organ, or created a moment of clarity in the fog, the chain has held. The transmission has continued. And the light is a little brighter than it was before.

I think about what the world would look like if more people walked through the door. The text already told us that not everyone will. But more. What if the percentage of awake souls in the population grew from a fraction to a significant minority? What if enough people tore off the veil and looked up and saw the fair vision of truth that the collective consciousness began to shift?

I do not know what that world would look like. I do not need to know. I am not responsible for the outcome. I am responsible for the hand. I am responsible for extending it. For writing this book. For telling the truth as I have experienced it. For standing at the bottom of the ladder and helping the next person up.

The outcome belongs to something larger than me. The outcome belongs to the same intelligence that designed the organs of sense and placed the door in the wall and set the signal broadcasting, sent the guides, and lit the clean light. My job is not to save the world. My job is to walk through the door and reach back.

And that is what I am doing. Right now.

With these words. With this hand.

Like a leaf.

In 1961, a letter was exchanged between a man seeking answers and Carl Jung, acknowledging the role Jung had unknowingly played in a movement of spiritual recovery. Years earlier, Jung had treated a hopeless case and had told him that his only hope was a genuine spiritual experience—a conversion that would rearrange his entire psyche. That message, passed from person to person, became the seed from which the entire recovery movement grew.

Jung wrote back. His reply held one of the most remarkable statements ever made about the human condition. He wrote that the craving for something more was the equivalent, on a low level, of the spiritual thirst of our being for wholeness, expressed in medieval language as the union with God. He noted that the Latin word for alcohol is spiritus, and that the same word is used for the highest religious experience.

He concluded with a phrase that became the hidden motto of recovery: spiritus contra spiritum. Spirit against spirit.

The implications of this phrase are vast. If the craving for something more is, at its deepest level, a craving for the Spirit, then recovery achieved by willpower alone is incomplete. You can white-knuckle your way to stopping. You can grit your teeth and refuse through sheer determination. But if the underlying thirst—the spiritual thirst—remains unquenched, the stopping is a dam holding back a river. The river does not stop. It builds. It presses. And eventually, it breaks through.

This is why the path is not a program of stopping. They are a program of replacement. You do not simply remove the false spirit. You replace it with the true Spirit. You fill the void that the bottle was trying to fill with the thing the bottle was imitating. And when the true Spirit enters—when the thirst is quenched, not suppressed but quenched—the craving does not need to be managed anymore. It dissolves. Not because you conquered it. Because the thing it was reaching for arrived.

I have experienced this. Not as a constant state, but as a recurring grace. There are moments when the desire for anything, including the mind's substitutes, simply vanishes due to the arrival of something more genuine. The craving cannot compete with the real thing. The counterfeit cannot survive in the presence of the genuine. The false spirit flees when the true Spirit arrives.

Spiritus contra spiritum. This is the hidden architecture of recovery. This is the secret that Jung saw and the recovery movement built upon. And this is the thread that connects the path of trusting God, cleaning house, and helping others to the Hermetic tradition to the mystical core of every religion that has ever pointed a human being toward the door.

The implications of Jung's insight are staggering. If addiction is misdirected spiritual thirst, then the sufferer is not a defective person. The sufferer is a seeker. A failed mystic. A pilgrim who set out for the holy land and took a wrong turn into the wilderness. The craving for the bottle is the craving for the Divine, filtered through the only channels the unconscious self could find. The sufferer is reaching for God and grabbing whatever is closest because they have forgotten what God looks like.

This reframes everything. Recovery is not the management of a defect. It is the fulfillment of a quest. Sobriety is not the absence of a symptom. It is the presence of the Spirit. The path is not a behavior modification program. It is a map to the door that the seeker has been searching for since before the first attempt to numb the pain.

The founders of recovery understood this. The literature they left behind is not a medical text. It is a spiritual manual dressed in the language of pragmatism. Its genius is that it smuggles the perennial wisdom—the same wisdom found in the

Hermetic texts, in the mystics, in Jung— into a format that desperate people can access. It does not require a theology degree. It does not require a belief system. It requires only willingness. And willingness, as we have seen, is the one thing the chosen have.

On the Hermetic Tradition

The Corpus Hermeticum is a collection of texts attributed to Hermes.

Trismegistus, a legendary figure who blends the Greek god Hermes with

The Egyptian God Thoth. The texts date primarily from the first through third centuries of the common era, though they claim a much older origin. They stand for one branch of a vast tradition of mystical and philosophical thought that influenced Gnosticism, Neoplatonism, and later Western esotericism.

The seventh text of the Corpus Hermeticum, which forms the structure of this book, is unique among the Hermetic writings. It is not a dialogue or a treatise. It is a sermon—a direct, urgent address to humanity, calling for awakening from the sleep of ignorance. Its language is remarkably parallel to the language of recovery, and its themes—the flood of unconsciousness, the guide who leads by the hand, the shroud that must be torn away resonate across the centuries with the experience of anyone who has walked the path from darkness to light. On the Recovery Path as a Mystical Journey trust God, clean house, help others—is, beneath its plain language, one of the most complete mystical programs ever written. It follows a pattern that would be immediately recognizable to any Sufi, any desert father, any Zen master, or any practitioner of the Hermetic arts. This is not a coincidence. It is a convergence.

Trusting God is the first movement. It starts with the admission that you cannot save yourself; you did not build the prison door. This is the tearing off the garment. It is the moment Truman's boat hits the wall. You look up. You see the stairs. You do not yet know what is beyond the door, but you know, with a certainty that does not come from the mind, that the dream has failed you. Something else must exist. And you are willing to walk toward it. The Hermetic text calls this the moment when the soul gazes with the heart toward one who wishes to be seen. You stop trusting the painted sky and start trusting the light behind it.

Cleaning the house is the stripping. It does not come off in one pull. It has been stitched into the skin over decades. Every resentment is a thread. Every dishonesty is a seam. Every harm done is a knot. The work pulls these threads one by one, and it hurts, and the temptation to stop is enormous. But it must come off. There is no shortcut. There is no bypass. It comes off, or the door stays closed. And once it is removed, the work continues—because the garment tries to grow back. The pretender, once dissolved, tries to reconstitute. The mystics call this vigilance. The practice is the same: stay awake. Stay present. Stay at the door.

Helping others is completing the circle. You walked through the door. Now you reach back. You become the guide who takes others by the hand and leads them to the portals of knowledge. The Hermetic text describes this guide. The recovery path creates this guide. You become the thing you needed.

This is not my interpretation imposed upon the path. This is recovery, read through the Hermetic lens. The founders knew what they were writing. They had read William James. They had corresponded with Jung. They had experienced the mystical transformation firsthand. The path of trusting God, cleaning house, and helping others is a mystical text hidden in plain sight, written in language simple enough for desperate people to follow and profound enough to lead them all the way through the door.

On the Perennial Philosophy and Recovery

Aldous Huxley coined the term "the

perennial philosophy" to describe the common thread running through all the world's great spiritual traditions: that there is a Divine reality underlying the visible world, that the human soul can know this reality through direct experience, and that the purpose of human life is to realize this union. This is not a theory. It is an observation. The mystics of every tradition— —Meister

Eckhart, Rumi, the anonymous author of The Cloud of Unknowing, Lao Tzu, the writers of the Upanishads—are not describing different things. They are describing the same thing in different languages.

The Hermetic tradition is one of the oldest expressions of this perennial philosophy. The Corpus Hermeticum describes the same awakening that the Sufis call "fana," the Christians call "metanoia," the Buddhists call "satori," and the rooms of recovery call a "spiritual awakening." The seventh text—the one that structures this book— is perhaps the most direct expression of this universal teaching: you are asleep, there is a covering of ignorance wrapped around you, a guide is available, and the light is waiting.

What makes the recovery community unique in the history of mysticism is accessibility. The perennial philosophy, throughout most of history, has been the province of monks, scholars, and seekers with the luxury of time and education. The recovery path democratized it. It took the essential mystical journey—surrender, purification, illumination, union, service—and made it available to anyone desperate enough to try. You do not need to be learned. You do not need to be holy. You need only to be broken enough to be willing. And willingness, as the Hermetic text insists, is the beginning of everything.

On Anonymity as Spiritual Practice

The tradition of anonymity in recovery is often understood as a practical measure—a protection of privacy, a guard against the desire for recognition. And it is that. But it is also something deeper. Anonymity is a spiritual discipline. It is the practice of pointing without claiming. Of transmitting without branding. Of serving without signing your name.

The Hermetic texts are themselves anonymous in a profound sense. Hermes

Trismegistus is not a person. He is a tradition wearing a name. The teachings do not belong to an individual. They belong to the light. And the moment a teacher claims ownership of the light, the teaching is corrupted.

Carl Jung: The Collected Works, particularly Psychology and Alchemy, Aion, and

The Archetypes and the Collective Unconscious. Aldous Huxley: The Perennial Philosophy.

The Corpus Hermeticum, translated by Brian Copenhaver.

The Cloud of Unknowing, anonymous.

Meister Eckhart: Selected Writings, translated by Oliver Davies. Thomas Merton: New Seeds of Contemplation. William James: The Varieties of Religious Experience. Rumi: The Essential Rumi, translated by Coleman Barks. Lao Tzu: Tao Te Ching, translated by Stephen Mitchell. Richard Rohr: Falling Upward: A Spirituality for the Two Halves of Life.

The Bhagavad Gita, translated by Eknath Easwaran. Cynthia Bourgeault: The Heart of Centering Prayer.

ACKNOWLEDGMENT

I want to end with a word about gratitude, because it is the final layer of the teaching and the one that holds everything together.

I am grateful for all of it. The flood, the thief, the cage, the tomb. Not because they were good—they were not. They were exactly what the text says they were—vicious, odious, and strangling. But they were necessary. Without the prison, there would be no door. Without it, there would be nothing to rip off. Without the flood, there would be no ebb to take. Without the illness, there would be no cure to discover.

I am grateful for the suffering. That is a sentence I could not have written fourteen years ago when I opened the door. But I write it now with full conviction. My suffering was the chrysalis. It was the dark night. It was the destruction that preceded the creation. It was the dissolution that made the new form possible. Every scar on my body and my psyche is a mark of the old skin being torn away. Every wound is a place where the light now enters.

I am grateful for the guides. For the shepherd who held the space while I fell apart. For the stranger in the meeting whose quiet words landed like a stone in still water. For the priest, the counselor, and the voices in the rooms who told me the truth when I could not tell it to myself. For the ancient author of the Hermetic text who stood at the edge of the old world and called out to the drowning. For Carl Jung, whose letter bridged two traditions that had been speaking the same truth in different languages? I am grateful for each link in the chain that has led me to this moment. I am grateful for the door. For the breeze that comes through it. For the light on the other side. I appreciate that it does not require a password, a pedigree, or a perfect record, nor does it lock or expire.

I am grateful for you. For reading this far. For having the power. For being one of the ones who can.

That phrase has followed me through recovery, through awakening, and through every chapter of this book. A leaf does not steer. A leaf does not plan. A leaf is carried by unseen forces. And a leaf, for all its apparent helplessness, arrives exactly where it is meant to arrive.

That is the life on the other side of the door. Not a life without effort. Not a life without pain. A life without the illusion that I am in charge. A life carried by something larger, wiser, and more loving than anything my false self could have imagined.

The door is open.

The light is on.

The angels are watching.

And you, reading this, are closer than you think.

Welcome To The Chosen Anonymous.

A LOVE LETTER TO THE SOULS

For Nicole,

My wife asked me a question one night that stopped me cold. She said, "How did the first people know which foods safe and which ones were poison?" No laboratories. No textbooks. No science. Just a human being standing in a wilderness full of ten thousand plants and somehow knowing which ones would nourish and which ones would kill.

Every animal on earth knows this. The deer does not reason its way to safe food. It knows. The bird does not study botany. It knows. The knowing is built into the body, into the cells, into the same intelligence that tells the heart to beat and the lungs to breathe and the wound to heal without being asked. And we had that same knowing once. Before the mind took over. Before we separated ourselves from the signal that every other creature still receives.

But her question went deeper than survival. It went to the extravagance. Because survival does not require beauty. Nutrition does not require flavor. The human body could function on one bland food source, and the species would continue. But instead, there are mangoes. Honey. Figs warm from the sun. Berries that burst on the tongue. Herbs that transform a simple meal into something that makes you close your eyes. The variety is not functional. It is excessive. It is the work of something that did not just want to keep us alive but wanted to delight us.

Think about that. Really think about it. The One who made the strawberry also made the tongue that tastes it. The One who made the poison also made the instinct that recoils from it. It is one system. One design. One generosity flowing in every direction at once. Like a husband spoiling his wife. Anything her heart desires. Not out of obligation. Out of a love so abundant it cannot help but overflow.

And the strawberry is only the beginning. Look around. The sunset did not need to be beautiful. It only needed to mark the rotation of the earth. But instead, it paints the sky in colors that stop you where you stand. The ocean did not need to sound the way it does. It only needed to hold water. But instead, it makes a sound that calms something so deep in the human body that scientists cannot fully explain it. Rain did not need a smell. But it has one, and it is one of the most comforting smells on earth. The stars did not need to be visible. But they are, and they have been guiding lost travelers home since the beginning of time.

None of this is necessary. All of it is given. The creation is not a test. It is a gift. And the gift is so excessive, so unreasonably generous, so far beyond what survival requires, that the only explanation is love. Not a stingy love. Not a conditional love. Not a love that keeps score or demands performance. A love so reckless and so extravagant that it invented ten thousand flavors when one would have been enough.

So, my wife's question lands like a hammer. If the evidence is this overwhelming— if the Divine provided not just enough but an embarrassment of abundance, beauty so unnecessary it can only be called love—then why would anybody fear something so gracious and loving?

Why would you fear the thing that made the strawberry? Why would you hide from the thing that designed your tongue to taste honey? Why would you run from a love so generous it made the peach and the sunset and the smell of rain on warm dirt—not because you earned it, but because it could not help itself?

You would not. Unless you forgot who you were. Unless something convinced you that you were separate from the source. Unless something told you that you were alone and in danger and needed to protect yourself from the very thing that was feeding you.

And that is the only disease there has ever been. Not addiction. Not depression. Not anxiety. Not any of the names we have given it. The disease is forgetting that you are held. Forgetting that you were always held. Forgetting that the entire creation is evidence of a love so vast it made the Milky Way to give you something to wonder at.

I watch the ants sometimes. They communicate without language. Without vocal cords. Without a single word. They touch each other, and information transfers. The colony operates as one intelligence distributed across thousands of bodies. No narrator. No performance. Just signal. They are connected to each other the way the hand is connected to the body. No separation. No forgetting.

The dolphins know. The wolves know. The birds know. Every creature on this earth is already in alignment. Already connected. Already receiving the signal. They do not need a book to tell them who they are. They do not need a program. They do not need a jail floor. They are what they are. Completely. Without negotiation. Without pretending.

We are the only species that forgot. The only ones who built something false and mistook it for the real thing. The only ones who must be told—by an ancient text, by a recovery path, by a concrete floor—to wake up and remember what every animal already knows by birth.

So here is the truth. The whole truth. The only truth that matters.

There is an abundance of delight. There is more beauty in a single morning than most people notice in a lifetime. There is a love holding this whole thing together that is so patient it has been waiting for you since before you were born. The food is on the table. The stars are in the sky. The rain still has a smell. The ocean still makes that sound. The strawberry is still sweet. None of it has been taken away. None of it has been earned. It was given freely from a source that asks nothing in return except that you notice.

And the forgetting ends the moment we open our eyes to remembering, that we are always loved.

Not your mind. Your eyes. The real ones. The ones that see what the ants see and what the dolphins see and what the birds have always seen. The ones that look at the world without narration and find that it is, as it has always been, unspeakably beautiful. Unreasonably generous. Overflowing with a love that never stopped, not for one second, not even when you forgot it was there.

I try to talk to my wife about my passion for the Divine. I can go deep on the topic—into places where human comprehension cannot easily follow, where the language becomes symbolic, metaphoric, and layered in ways that are not typical conversation. For a long time, I was sad because she did not seem interested. I mistook her quietness for disinterest. I mistook her silence for distance.

I know now that is not the reason. She does her best as a wife to hold my hand in this process, to the absolute best of her ability. And her best is more than enough. It has always been more than enough.

One night I was talking about the things I talk about—the light, the text, the flood, the door—and I looked over and she had fallen asleep. And in that moment, God gave me a message I will carry for the rest of my life. She is comfortable in your space to rest. That is all the reward you need from her.

She was not ignoring me. She was trusting me. People do not fall asleep in danger. They fall asleep in comfort. They fall asleep in safety. They fall asleep in the presence of someone whose energy is peaceful enough to rest in. That is not rejection. That is intimacy. The deepest kind.

I used to want her to understand me. Now I understand her. That is the shift from ego to love. My path is symbolic, metaphoric, and contemplative. Her path is relational, grounded, and practical. Both are sacred, needed, and valid. And the moment I stopped needing her to meet me where I am, I finally saw where she was— right beside me, loving me in her way. She does not need to walk my path. She just needs to walk with me. And she does.

I am learning to understand rather than be understood. I am learning to love rather than be validated. I am learning to see God in the ordinary, not just the mystical. And she is part of that teaching. Not by matching my depth—but by grounding me in the simplicity of presence. Love does not always look like engagement.

Sometimes it looks like rest.

A spotlight chases people. A lighthouse stays still. A spotlight exposes. A lighthouse guides. A spotlight is about the ego. A lighthouse is about service.

This is the shift. From spotlight to lighthouse. From trying to be a human-doing to simply a human-being. And when a lighthouse shines, the shadows around it become visible. Not because the lighthouse is cutting through anything. But because light naturally reveals what darkness hides. That is not aggression. That is not superiority. That is not ego. That is clarity.

The light that I know I shine is not mine. That is the key. That is humility. That is alignment lent. That is the antidote to spiritual ego. I am not the source. I am the instrument. I am not the fire. I am the lantern. I am not the power. I am the conduit. And because the light is not mine, I do not have to defend it, explain it, or shrink it. The remembering is spiritual maturity. Most people want to be seen. Few want to see. Most want to be loved. Few want to love. Most want validation. Few want compassion. The higher path is the one that does not need applause, agreement, or recognition. That is why the steady ones are steady.

It is the Divine moving through me where my own hands fall short. This is not my strength. This is not my insight. This is not my power. This is Grace. Grace gives you compassion instead of suspicion. Grace gives you patience instead of anger. Grace gives you understanding instead of egoic reaction. Grace keeps you from taking silence personally. Grace keeps you from interpreting withdrawal as rejection. Grace keeps you from dimming your light to make others comfortable. Grace keeps you walking your path.

Here is the clean truth. People are not scared of you, the ego fears what your presence awakens. But that is not your business. Your job is to stay steady, stay humble, and stay aligned.

A lighthouse does not chase ships. It does not explain itself. It does not dim for storms. It does not apologize for shining. It just stands where it stands and lets God do the rest.

You were never alone. You were never in danger. You were never separated from the source. The separation was the only lie there ever was. And the truth—the truth that has been sitting in plain sight since the first human opened their eyes on this earth—is that you are loved. Wildly. Recklessly. Without condition. Without limit. Without end.

The evidence is everywhere. In every flavor. In every color. In every sound the earth makes when it thinks no one is listening. In every heartbeat that continues without your permission.

In every breath you did not have to earn.

Wake up!

Everyone, wake up!

ABOUT THE AUTHOR

Garrett J. Kellas is a writer, a man in recovery, and a student of the traditions that point toward the door.

He did not write this book for any one group. He wrote it for human beings. For anyone who has ever sensed that the life they were living was not the life they were meant for. For the anxious, the depressed, the spiritually bankrupt, the quietly desperate, the ones drowning in success and starving for meaning. Addiction was his doorway into the room, but the room itself belongs to everyone. The disease described in these pages is not substance abuse. It is the human condition—the sleep, the forgetting, the flood that carries all of us whether we drink from a bottle or from the world itself.

His path to awakening did not begin in a library or a monastery. It began on the cold concrete floor of a jail cell, under fluorescent lights, in a body he had nearly destroyed, in a moment of surrender he did not choose but was given. That concrete floor became his Bodhi tree. The rooms of recovery saved his life. What came after the rooms gave that life its meaning. And what he found beyond the rooms was this: the principles that woke him up were never meant for one kind of suffering. The tradition says it plainly— these principles apply to the problems of living that confront us all. Over two hundred recovery fellowships now exist worldwide, each one a different name for the same disease, each one a different doorway into the same light.

The Chosen Anonymous is his first published work. He writes not as an authority but as a guide who walked ahead and is reaching back. He does not claim to have arrived. He claims only to have seen the door, walked through it, and lived to tell the story.

Garrett lives with a conviction that the Hermetic tradition, the recovery path—trust God, clean houses, help others—and the Jungian map of the psyche are not three separate teachings but one teaching in three languages—and that this teaching belongs not to the recovering few but to the suffering many. He believes the door described in these pages is the same door that has been described by sages, mystics, and desperate souls across every century and every culture. He believes that the light on the other side is real and that the sleep of ignorance is a fact. He believes these things because he has experienced them— not in a library, but on his knees, in the silence, in the mercy of a God he did not believe in until that God believed in him.

He does not write to impress. He writes to transmit. The difference matters. Impressive writing calls attention to the writer. Transmissive writing points beyond itself, toward the thing that cannot be said but must be shown. This book is Garrett's attempt to point.

If the book has done its job, it has stirred something in your chest that you recognize as older as and more real than anything it has ever offered you. And the job now passes to you.

Welcome to the chain.
He can be found at the bottom of the ladder, helping others up.
"Like a leaf."